CUMBRIA'S PREHISTORIC MONUMENTS

When stone speaks,
just listen.

Let rain wash words
to sore soil.

Let sun bake old time;
tomes of bones.

Let lichen's text come
and grow.

– 'Unnamed Megalith',
Simon De Courcey

First published 2021
Reprinted with amendments, 2022, 2024

The History Press
The Mill, Brimscombe Port
Stroud, Gloucestershire, GL5 2QG
www.thehistorypress.co.uk

Photos and diagrams by the author.

British Library Cataloguing in Publication Data.
A catalogue record for this book is available from the British Library.

ISBN 978 0 7509 9668 6

Typesetting and origination by Typo•glyphix, Burton-on-Trent
Printed by TJ Books Limited, Padstow, Cornwall

CUMBRIA'S PREHISTORIC MONUMENTS

Written & illustrated by

ADAM MORGAN IBBOTSON

CONTENTS

INTRODUCTION

Britain's prehistoric monuments offer a unique glimpse into the lives and religious customs of Europe's earliest settled communities. They are the remnants of the cultures that inhabited the British Isles during two distinct periods: the Neolithic and the Bronze Age. These eras, which spanned between 4000 BC and 700 BC, could be considered a 'prehistoric golden age'. It was during this golden age, thousands of years before Roman sandals touched British shores, that some of Europe's grandest monuments were created.

Despite the global appreciation of Britain's prehistoric monuments, only a select few sites are generally known to the public. Stonehenge, for instance, has become a universally recognised mascot for the Stone Age, appearing in popular culture all around the globe. But while Stonehenge and its surrounding landscape are undoubtedly grand, many people are unaware that the best-preserved examples of such monuments exist at Britain's extremities. Among such areas are Cornwall, Scotland, Western Ireland, Wales and – as shown in this book – Cumbria.

Cumbria is the least densely populated county in England and is perhaps better recognised for its landscapes than its inhabitants. While Cumbria's cultural heritage may appear remote to some, its isolation has undoubtedly played a role in the preservation of monuments of extreme antiquity. Without the need to cram every corner of this land with housing developments, supermarkets or motorways, ancient monuments – the large and the small – have triumphantly survived over the millennia. They stand as resolute as they did thousands of years ago, time capsules to a world so different it can seem alien.

It is thanks to this remoteness that Cumbria has retained some of the most breathtaking prehistoric monuments in the world, a combination of massive stones and stunning views. Places with this level of historical importance are seldom found among such beauty. Yet here, from the fells of the Lake District to the shores of the Irish Sea, you can find yourself alone with nothing but a stunning view and an ancient stone monument. For those who have experienced the droves of tourists that accompany any visit to Stonehenge, this seclusion will doubtlessly be appreciated.

In this book you will find an assortment of monuments, some on the tourist trail and others that are virtually unexplored. You may find that the best sites lie off the beaten track, in the most unexpected areas, which is terrific if you enjoy an adventure into the unfamiliar. I invite you to take a journey thousands of years back into our past, to an era sculpted by ancient hands.

These are ***Cumbria's Prehistoric Monuments.***

A QUICK GUIDE BEFORE YOU START

Since the eighteenth century, academic institutions across Europe have worked tirelessly to help further our understanding of Britain's prehistoric past. When we are looking at what are essentially just stone arrangements, we must find a way to differentiate between them. Therefore, a jargon all its own has emerged. Take the paragraph below as an example:

> *A menhir stands at the centre of the henge monument, next to which is a small Bronze Age round cairn. Decorated with intricate cup marks, its position at the end of the avenue makes it the perfect spot to gaze out onto the cairn-field*

If you understood this paragraph, congratulations; you should turn the page and continue. But for the uninitiated – please take note of this small glossary.

Term	Definition
bell beaker	A non-funerary pottery vessel dating to the Early Bronze Age, typically 12–30 cm tall with a fluted top.
burial cairn	A mound of stones created to mark burials.
burial circle	A stone circle with a central burial cairn.
cairn field	An expanse of land with several prehistoric cairns.
cap stone	A stone that covers a cist burial.
cist	A small stone-built, coffin-like box or ossuary used to hold the bodies of the dead. Typically found within burial cairns.
collared urn	A Bronze Age urn with a heavy overhanging rim or collar.
concentric stone crcle	A stone circle encircling another stone circle.
crag	A steep or rugged cliff or rock face.
crop marks	Patterns found in grown crops. This is due to differing levels of growth caused by historical changes to the bedrock.
cup and ring marks	A style of rock art typical of the Neolithic, consisting of chiselled rings and dots on a rockface.
flint	A sedimentary form of quartz used throughout the Stone Age to sculpt cutting tools.
henge	An earthwork typical of the Neolithic period, consisting of a roughly circular or oval-shaped bank with an internal ditch surrounding a central flat area.
hut circle	The foundation of a prehistoric roundhouse, typically circular stone walls with a cobbled interior.
kerb stones	A row of stones forming a kerb, holding a mound of stone or earth in place around its outside.
lynchet	A ridge or ledge formed along the downhill side of a plot by ploughing in ancient times.

Term	Definition
menhir	A standing stone erected with human agency, typically dating from the Neolithic through to the Bronze Age.
microlith	A minute shaped flint, typically part of a composite tool such as a spear.
polished axe	A well-honed stone axe typically dating to the Neolithic period, although earlier examples have been found.
portal stones	A term used to define large stones that appear to form an entrance.
solstice	The time of year when the sun reaches its highest point. This occurs twice a year, in summer and winter, marking both the longest and shortest days of the year.
stone avenue	Two rows of stone running parallel through the landscape.
stone circle	A circular arrangement of stones.
stone row	A single row of stones which forms a line in the landscape.
survivor bias	A logical error made by concentrating on things that survive today, in ignorance of non-surviving examples.
tumulus / tumuli	Any variety of mound intended to inter the dead.
cremation cemetary	An area where bodies were cremated and buried, either in coffins or cists.

Mound Variety	Description
kerbed cairn	A style of burial monument common in the Bronze Age (2500–1500 BC). A small circle of stones encases a flattened mound of earth.
bowl barrow	An earth-covered tomb which gets its name from its resemblance to an upturned bowl.
long barrow	A long earthen tumulus with a stone chamber in one end. Often described as 'chambered tombs'. Typically made during the Neolithic (4000–2500 BC).

Mound Variety	Description
passage tomb	A type of barrow that has a narrow access passage made of large stones. Typically made during the Neolithic (4000–2500 BC).
round cairn	Large stone mounds covering single or multiple burials. Typically made during the Bronze Age (2500–800 BC).
clearance cairn	An uneaven heap of stones removed from farmland. Does not contain burials.

Throughout this book the author will be explaining the historical context behind these sites and offering an explanation behind their proposed functions. There may be times it is necessary to refer to this glossary, and that is without shame. Despite appearing crude on their surface, these monuments are vestiges of a complex prehistoric society we have yet to fully understand.

Often, prehistoric monuments are situated in areas that are hard to access, be it physically or legally. This book serves to inform the reader of the extent of the prehistoric monuments in Cumbria, and is not an invitation to trespass or disrupt any of the areas detailed in its pages.

THE NEOLITHIC: 4200 BC–2500 BC

Neo / *new or of recent manufacture.*

Lithic / *of the nature of or relating to stone.*

There has been much debate about what defines the British Neolithic, and when the period began. The predominant theory is that a population of people from mainland Europe migrated to England around 4200 BC, bringing with them innovative farming techniques, fixed human settlements and complex religious systems. Simply put, the Neolithic was a period of the Stone Age during which people became more settled in the landscape.

The monument types that define British prehistory derive from the Neolithic. Stone circles and burial cairns emerged during this period, and earthworks such as 'henge monuments' were created on a grand scale, often accompanying megalithic sites. Many of these traditions carried over into the Bronze Age, which can make Neolithic sites difficult to date based on appearance alone. However, several key distinctions can be made in Cumbria. It is a period that saw the construction of vast religious enclosures, created by arranging large boulders. Rock art sites are also an indicator of the Neolithic period, when cup and ring designs were a particularly common motif.

Stone tools are among the most striking artifacts of the period. They are often accidentally unearthed by landowners and are generally isolated finds. These tools can vary significantly in shape and size, from bulbous hammers to streamlined axe heads. Unlike arrowhead discoveries, often linked to the earlier Stone Age periods, these larger tool heads are evidence of a more domestic lifestyle.

The end of the Neolithic is often referred to as the 'Early Bronze Age' or 'Late Neolithic', a crucially important time in European prehistory. Neolithic farming communities saw a dramatic collapse during this transition, and up to 90 per cent of the British population may have been replaced by European migrants. Whether this was caused by famine, disease or genocide is not understood, but the genetics of these earlier people were all but eradicated in some areas. Nevertheless, stone circles approximately dating to the Early Bronze Age are often complex. Sites such as Stonehenge began their construction during the Neolithic, but had their stones rearranged during the Early Bronze Age. Alignments towards the solstice sun were also prevalent at this time, which can be seen at several sites across Cumbria.

The Neolithic was the foundation for our modern world. Culture began with innovation, and with that came science, philosophy and art.

- A NEOLITHIC AXE HEAD FROM LANGDALE-

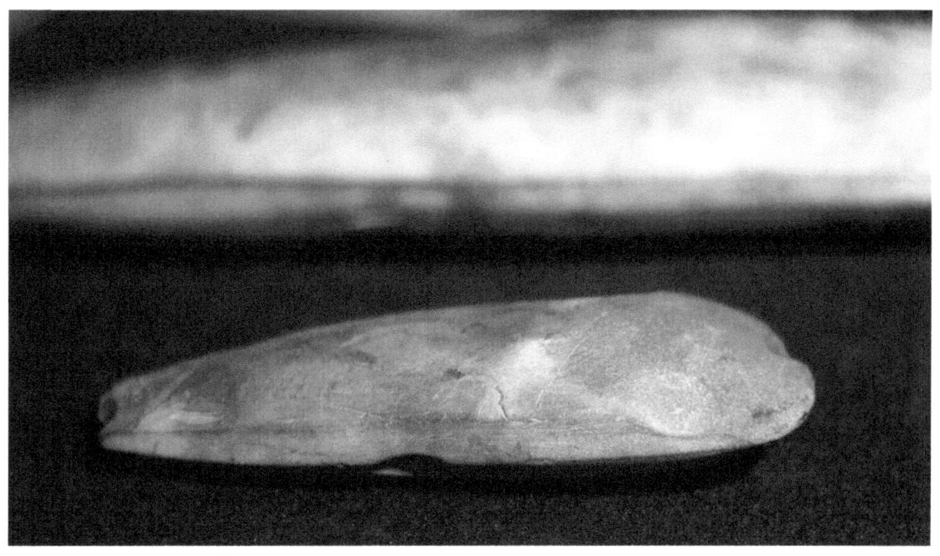

- A COLLECTION OF MICROLITHS DATING TO THE NEOLITHIC -

Before the discovery of metal working, the tools used to cut, scrape or hunt were entirely made of stone and wood.

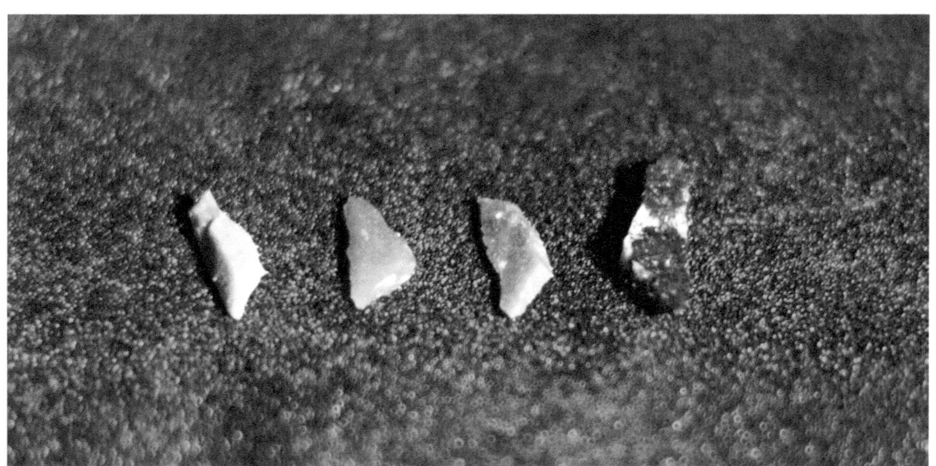

THE BRONZE AGE: 2500 BC–700 BC

Bronze / *an alloy metal consisting primarily of copper and tin.*

Age / *a distinct period of history.*

The Bronze Age followed directly on from the Neolithic, around 2500 BC. It marked the end of the Stone Age, and the start of a major development of cultural ideas across Britain. This was not a set moment in time, more a gradual shift in ideas as metallurgy spread across Europe via invasions and trade. Although the name implies that this was a time marked by the use of bronze, the Bronze Age is better explained as the period in which people began to produce metals, leading to a boom in bronze, copper and gold production. Stone tools were replaced with metal, and the process of working stone eventually vanished.

The period following the Neolithic/Early Bronze Age saw a gradual increase in individual burials. Unlike earlier graves, which tended to contain the bones of several people, Middle Bronze Age graves usually contain single cremated burials placed within urns. Researchers have conflicting opinions on the reasoning behind this. Some believe that this was due to the emergence of 'chieftains' who, like Egyptian pharaohs, were given their own burial monuments. Others argue that new religious rituals played a larger role, with burial accessories becoming especially important to Bronze Age people.

Most prehistoric pottery, weapons and jewellery artifacts date to the Bronze Age, and highly decorated urns are a common indicator of a site belonging to this period. These burial vessels came in numerous shapes and sizes. Typically, they were taller than they were wide, and displayed geometric motifs carved into their sides. Additional pottery known as beakers also became common in the Bronze Age, and were tightly linked to the so called Beaker People.

The Beaker People migrated to England around 2500 BC, right at the end of the Neolithic period, possibly kickstarting the Early Bronze Age in Britain. Despite their strong ties to their respective style of pottery, nobody knows the purpose of their beakers. They did not contain cremated remains, but were instead buried next to the deceased. Curiously, complete beakers are rarely found in Cumbria, and are more commonly found in southern England and northern Scotland.

The Bronze Age was, perhaps, the period in which personal possessions became essential to one's social standing. Possibly spurred on by the discovery of precious metals, Bronze Age people began to decorate themselves, their tools and even their tombs with decorative trinkets. While their monuments became smaller, and focused on the personal rather than the community, the artifacts found within them are often luxurious and impressively ornate.

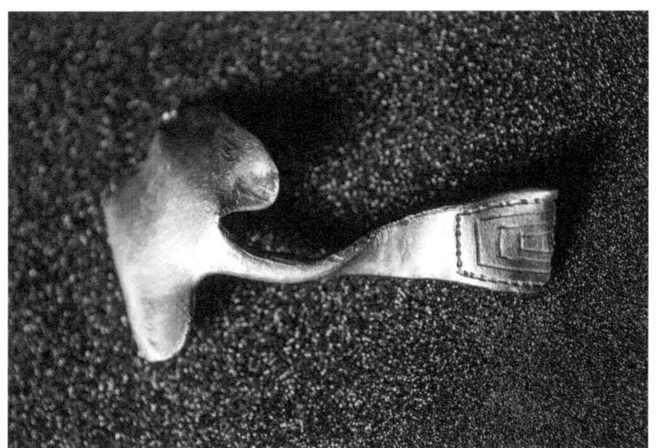

– A GOLDEN 'LUNULA' DATING TO THE BRONZE AGE –
One of only three fragments found in England. est. 2200–1700 BC, found during an archaeological dig near Bampton. Lunulas are typically found in mainland Europe and Ireland.

– AN INCENSE CUP DATING TO THE BRONZE AGE –
It is thought to have been an accessory to a burial, an item not intended to hold remains, but instead buried as a votive offering.

CHAPTER 1

THE CENTRAL LAKES

It is easy to see why millions of people flock to this UNESCO World Heritage Site every year. The Lake District is home to England's largest lakes and highest peaks, making it both a walker's paradise and a photographer's dream. This is, for obvious reasons, a region that has inspired artists for thousands of years, and the prehistoric sites here are believed to be among the oldest that the UK has to offer.

The long valleys and sheltering crags of the Lake District would have helped protect against all that nature could throw at the Neolithic people, and its plateaued moorlands would have been ideal for farming during the Bronze Age, when the climate was wetter. It may be for these reasons that prehistoric people would begin to venerate the fells of the Lake District.

These prehistoric landscapes are divided by England's tallest mountains, and despite their proximity, they can feel worlds apart. Take Troutbeck and Grasmere, for example. Only a spine of fells separates these two sweeping valleys, yet the prehistoric monuments found within them are remarkably different. To venture from valley to valley today only requires a five-minute drive, but without cars, roads or electronic maps, several hours of strenuous hiking would be required to journey between them. To put this into context with a modern equivalent: an hour's commute is the difference between living in Manchester or Liverpool, unarguably different settlements with their own distinct dialects and landmarks.

If you are interested in visiting a scenic environment with all the mod cons of a modern tourist destination, the Lake District may be the perfect place to explore some of Europe's finest prehistoric sites.

LANGDALE

ESTIMATED DATE OF OCCUPATION

4200 BC–3000 BC

The Great Langdale Valley extends 12,000 acres from Ambleside to the Mickelden Valley, passing through Skelwith Bridge, Elterwater and Chapel Stile.

When Britain entered the Neolithic period around 4000 BC, one of the biggest innovations was the popularisation of the polished stone axe. These axes were near perfectly honed, demonstrating a high level of technical skill. Their presence within a region indicates the settlement of Neolithic people and the existence of a nearby prehistoric trade network.

But where did they come from?

In the 1930s, several examples of such artifacts were traced to Langdale, hinting that this quiet valley hid an exciting secret. Langdale is now generally believed to represent the earliest indication of the Neolithic revolution in Cumbria. It was here that a stone axe industry is thought to have been in operation for over 500 years, from 3800 BC to 3200 BC – a considerable portion of the Neolithic period.

Axe heads originating from Langdale have been unearthed in North Yorkshire, Scotland, London and Ireland, suggesting Neolithic Cumbria was connected to the rest of Britain via trade networks, with Langdale axes being one of the foremost exports.

Langdale is perhaps the backbone, the true heart of innovation, for almost all prehistoric monuments across Cumbria.

– LANGDALE –

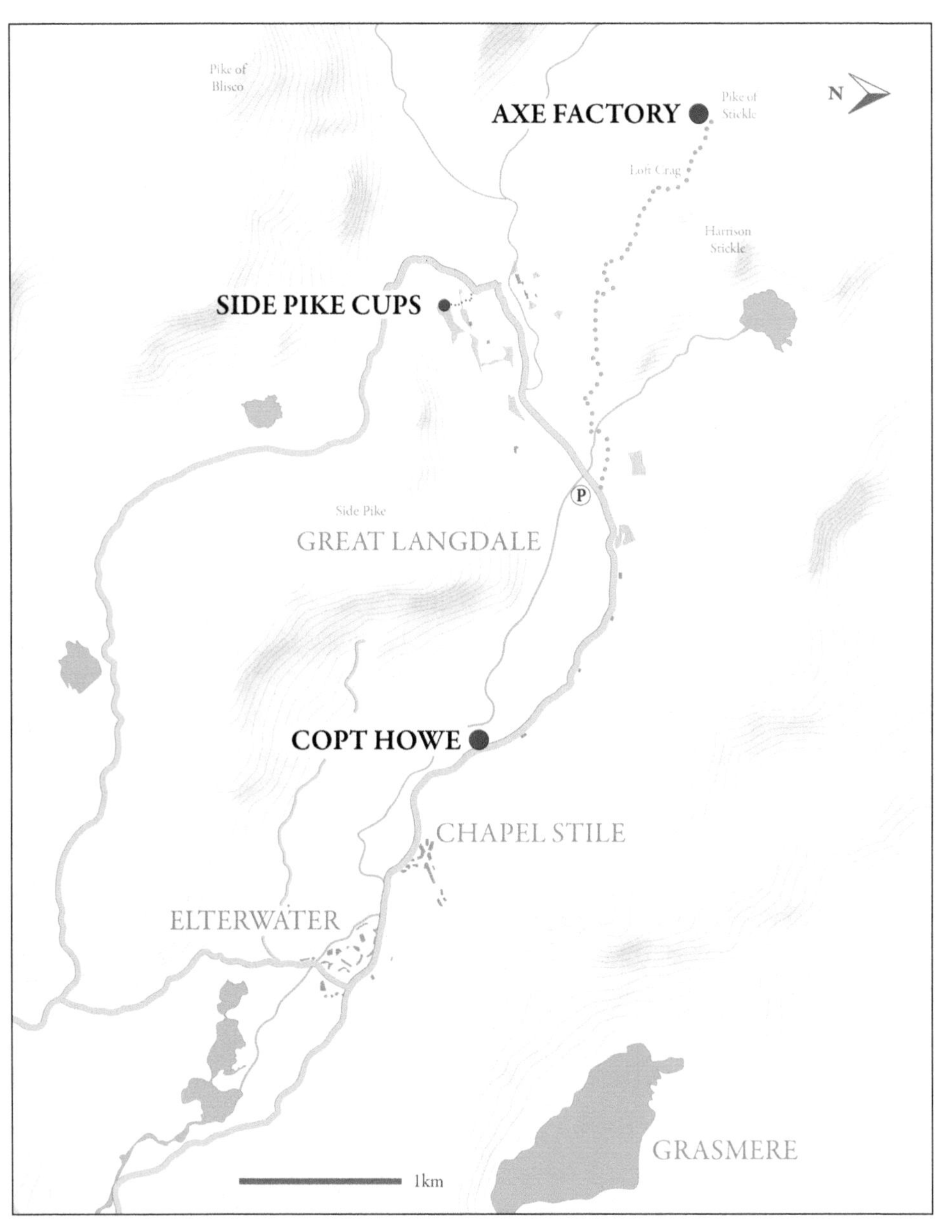

Pike of Blisco
AXE FACTORY
Pike of Stickle
N
Loft Crag
Harrison Stickle
SIDE PIKE CUPS
P
Side Pike
GREAT LANGDALE
COPT HOWE
CHAPEL STILE
ELTERWATER
GRASMERE
1km

THE AXE FACTORY

The Axe Factory, a collection of Neolithic quarries found across the Langdale Pikes, is estimated to have produced 21 per cent of all polished axe heads discovered throughout Britain. The Pikes and their surrounding area can be unstable and perilous, so make sure to be well prepared if you intend to visit.

The clearest physical evidence for the Axe Factory is a man-made cave on the Pike of Stickle; however, this was far from the only quarry. Worked stone outcrops have been identified all along the hills surrounding Langdale, and axe heads have been discovered on Harrison Stickle, Scafell Pike and Glamara. The stone was not only quarried here either. On Glamara and Harrison Stickle, indication of knapping has been found. This was the process of chiselling the raw stone into shape, creating semi-honed 'roughout' axe heads. Axes were likely traded as roughouts, then later honed by the communities who received them.

Since the 1930s, researchers have debated why people would climb these treacherous hills to quarry and knap. The same stone is both easier to source and more abundant elsewhere, yet the stone found at this location was evidently popular. The steep-sided fells would make Langdale a difficult place to traverse, and an even more challenging location for quarrying. Almost all the quarries are found on incredibly difficult terrain, near vertical drops, which begs the question: *Why Langdale?*

Despite the same greenstone appearing in easier to source locations, it is on a treacherous scree slope that we find the clearest indication of quarrying. It is for this reason that the axe heads are believed to have been sacred objects, with the toil involved in their sourcing possibly contributing to their value. If this was the case, then we can presume that these were driven, spiritual people, who venerated their landscapes. Their dedication to quarrying here highlights just how deep the connection between their landscape and their religious beliefs was – a crucial connection to understand when we study the prehistoric monuments of Cumbria.

– HARRISON STICKLE –

Once honed, Langdale axe heads were of astounding quality. Using a variety of honing techniques, they were polished to be made smooth, and the blade sharpened to a cutting point capable of felling trees. The weight of the head would have been enough to help automate the labour, and just relaxing your arm would have allowed for a satisfying and efficient swing.

Debate as to the purpose of polished axes is almost continuous. While they would make for practical tools, they are often found buried among graves and nearby stone circles. They were not jagged flints, nor were they crude lumps of rock – they were works of art, clearly created with their aesthetic value at the forefront of their design. Numerous axe varieties were created during the Neolithic period, some ceremonial, others for practical use; the polished axes traced to Langdale were cherished, and almost certainly created for ceremonial use.

Langdale axe heads are often discovered near water sources, such as the River Thames or Irish Sea. The Furness Peninsula, for instance, is a hotbed for axe head finds. During the Early Neolithic, much of Cumbria was covered in dense forest, making the land practically impassable by foot. Therefore, it is assumed that prehistoric Britons used boats, both over rivers and sea, becoming infamously gifted in seafaring by the time the Romans landed in AD 43. Some believe that an overseas trade route existed along Britain's coast, dispersing Langdale axe heads across Britain. This would explain how these Lake District axes ended up as far as Ireland and London.

Author's Notes: Several Langdale axe heads can be found in the British Museum, but closer to home you can find an excellent display of these axes at Keswick Museum, Kendal Museum and Tullie House Museum in Carlisle. Elsa Price, the Curator of Human History at Tullie House Museum & Art Gallery, gave me the opportunity to handle and photograph the beautifully crafted axe head pictured on page 13.

SIDE PIKE CUPS

This dimpled boulder sits in a patch of woodland just south of a National Trust campsite. Its distinctive shape makes it easy to identify between the numerous boulders that litter the area. The rock is not a standing stone, but instead a naturally situated boulder. It is green and bowl shaped, exhibiting twenty-three cup marks across its flat top.

Cup marks are small concave depressions, pecked into the surface of rocks. They date to the early-to-mid Neolithic (est. 3800–3000 BC), meaning that they were created using non-metallic tools. Various objects across Britain exhibit cup marks, some naturally situated, others erected by human hands. Stone circles, cairns, natural outcrops and burial chambers have been known to exhibit these curious motifs.

– SIDE PIKE CUPS –

One through-line connecting many cup marks is their proximity to Neolithic graves. If this was the case, this cup-marked rock may have been used as a form of burial marker, similar in purpose to a modern-day gravestone. This could suggest the presence of nearby burials.

Evidence of nearby prehistoric occupation was found at Blea Tarn, not far up the hill. Using pollen analysis, researchers verified that trees around the tarn were felled during the Neolithic period, evidence for agricultural land clearances. It is difficult to see now thanks to tree cover, but this plateaued area stands directly opposite the Langdale Pikes. With its commanding views over the Axe Factory, and its proximity to fresh flowing rivers, this would have been a desirable place to settle.

COPT HOWE

Copt Howe, the most complex canvas of prehistoric rock carvings in Cumbria, was only rediscovered in 1999. It is found on the Langdale Boulders, two naturally situated boulders at the south-east end of the Langdale Valley. Surprisingly, the best time to visit is at night, when you can reveal the carvings using a torch in the dark, which is the only way to see some of the more weathered motifs.

Cup and ring marks are found all across Western Europe, from Spain to Denmark, but they are especially common in northern England. This style of rock art consists of dense clusters of concentric circles and scraped-out cup marks. Only a few rock art sites are found across the Lake District, and those with ring markings are almost non-existent. Despite this, Copt Howe displays some of the largest and most complex ring mark motifs in Britain.

The meaning behind cup and ring marks is one of Britain's great archaeological conundrums. Found across a broad range of prehistoric sites, on natural rocks, stone circles and cairns, there is little consistency to their placement, aside from their occasional proximity to burials. Antiquarian William Greenwell believed they could have represented 'the most esoteric principle of the religion held by these people' – not unlike the Christian cross or Taoist Yin Yang.

– LANGDALE BOULDERS –

The meaning of Copt Howe is still open to interpretation. A popular theory suggests a portion of the art figuratively represents the Langdale Pikes, the location of the Langdale Axe Factory. Just scanning over the rockface, it is easy to conclude that it represents the sunset over the Pike of Stickle, with a large ring mark symbolising the sun. If we are to assume that this portion of the art represents the Langdale Pikes, it should be only natural that other areas of the carving are also figurative.

Unfortunately for those who believe this theory, which is temptingly simple, Neolithic art is rarely figurative. In fact, other than the ring markings, the carvings at Copt Howe bear little resemblance to the cup and ring motifs found commonly across England. Instead, the art here is far more in line with the abstract motifs etched onto Neolithic passage tombs in Ireland. Considering the long-range spread of Langdale axe heads during the Neolithic, this is not too unexpected. Trade routes overseas not only transported goods, but also culture. The reason why this complex example of Irish burial chamber art is found on the Langdale Boulders is, however, quite mysterious.

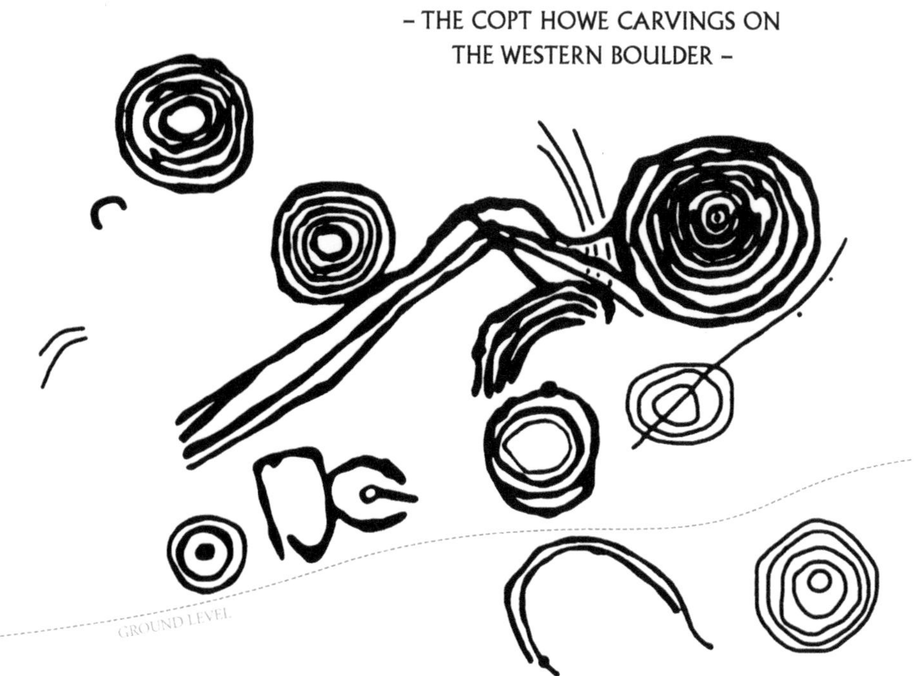

– THE COPT HOWE CARVINGS ON THE WESTERN BOULDER –

In 2018, archaeologists Richard Bradley, Aaron Watson and Peter Style (among others) excavated and surveyed the site, dating it between 3300 BC and 2900 BC. No burials were found during the dig, but numerous stone tools were unearthed at the base of the rock art.

Another connection between Copt Howe and passage tombs in Ireland was noted by the excavation team. Every summer solstice, when viewing the Langdale Pikes through the gap between the boulders, you can witness the sunset behind Harrison Stickle. Neolithic burial chambers, especially those in Ireland, often housed multiple bodies. Their large chambers served a practical purpose, storing the dead in a respectful manner, while adhering to certain religious principles (such as aligning their tombs towards the solstice sun). A perfectly formed natural passage like the Langdale Boulders, which aligns towards the summer solstice sun, would not have gone unnoticed by a Neolithic community.

The team theorised that the Langdale Boulders could have been used as a naturally formed portal into the Langdale Valley. No burial chamber necessarily existed here; the boulders would simply mimic the entrance to a Neolithic Irish tomb. Certainly, no Irish-style burial chambers exist at Copt Howe today, only the associated rock art; but as they say, there is no smoke without fire. We can assume that at least some funeral activity was taking place between the Langdale Boulders during the Neolithic period. Unfortunately, the boulders have been quarried over the past 400 years, heavily reducing the size of the easternmost boulder and our ability to comprehend it.

GRASMERE

ESTIMATED DATE OF OCCUPATION

3000 BC–Bronze Age (est. 1500 BC)

The area surrounding the village of Grasmere is one of the county's most popular tourist destinations. With iconic fells and lakes located nearby, like Helvellyn and Rydal Water, it is easy to see why Grasmere attracts so many visitors. However, despite residing on busy stretches of the tourist trail, the prehistoric sites here are lesser known and seldom visited when compared to other areas of Cumbria.

The remains of two distinct eras of prehistoric art can be found in the region. During the Neolithic period Stone Age people etched cup markings (like those found in Langdale) into the countless crags in the area. Hundreds of examples of prehistoric rock art likely once existed near Grasmere, but only a few surviving instances can be appreciated today. During the Bronze Age, moors such as Dunmail Raise were used as an area to cremate and bury the dead into cairns. This can be seen in several different forms, some large and grandiose, and others small and utilitarian.

Situated east of Grasmere are the two archaeologically rich valleys of Troutbeck and Rydal. They contain a host of Bronze Age ruins and settlements. Unlike nearby sites that are tied to the Neolithic period, the purpose of these Bronze Age monuments is better understood.

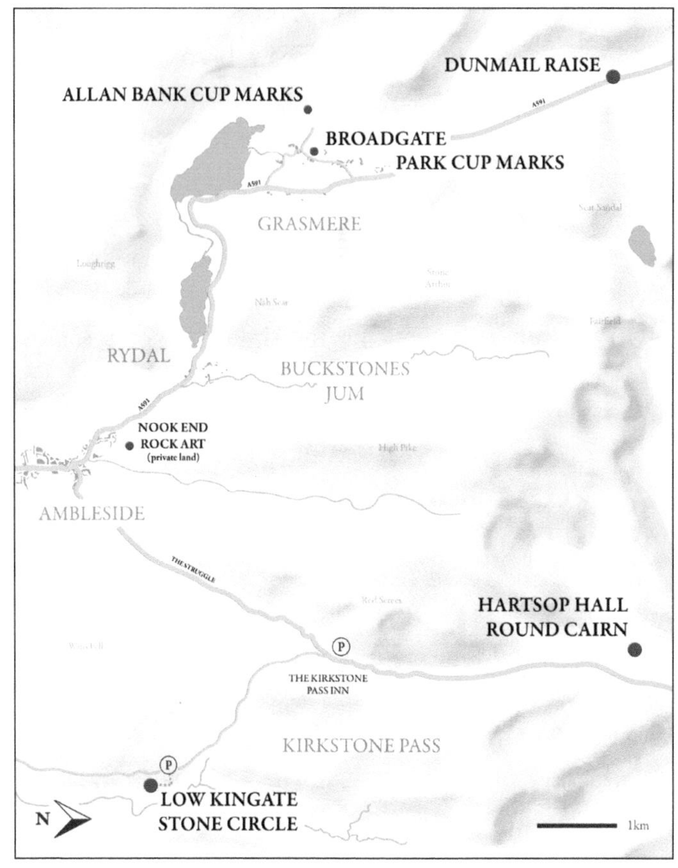

- GRASMERE -

GRASMERE CUPS

The search for rock art sites in the Lake District began in 1999, when an Ambleside resident uncovered a heavily cup-marked crag in his private garden. Rock art sites in the Lakes were once thought to be non-existent, so this discovery was unprecedented at the time. Since then, a significant collection of rock carvings has been identified within the Grasmere area, all formed in a distinct style. We will be focusing on just two.

The first of Grasmere's cup-marked rocks is located behind the Grasmere war memorial, on a small crag at the far end of Broadgate Park. Twenty cup marks were deeply carved into several parallel lines. The crag is now mostly covered by moss, but a large section of the art is clear enough to appreciate.

Another collection of cup marks is found surrounding Allan Bank, a Victorian house owned by the National Trust. Like at Broadgate Park, the cup markings are deeply etched into parallel lines, as well as circular arrangements. Several Langdale axes were unearthed in an adjacent field between two of the cup-marked crags. Therefore, activity in the area may go as far back as the Langdale Axe Factory, roughly between 3800 BC and 3200 BC.

– ALLAN BANK CUPMARKED ROCK –

Some researchers, such as archaeologist Peter Style, have drawn parallels between the Grasmere Cups and carvings found in Ireland. If this is the case, then the Grasmere Cups, like Copt Howe, may provide evidence for either a cultural influence or settlement of Irish people during the Neolithic period.

It will serve the reader well to remember that several prehistoric sites in Cumbria may be the work of migrant cultures. Sprinkles of foreign influence can be found at many prehistoric sites across the county, suggesting Cumbria was something of a cultural melting pot throughout prehistory. Given the abundance of Irish rock art in the Lake District, it may be obvious to assume Irish migrants were passing through the area.

Author's Notes: Since these sites are little known and scantly researched, it is unlikely that most rock faces around Grasmere have been checked for art. The chances are, much like the recently discovered rock carvings at Copt Howe, there are far more yet to find. If you do happen to stumble across any cup-marked rocks (which you are certain are authentic), be sure to report your discovery to the Lake District National Park Authorities.

– BROADGATE MEADOW ROCK ART –

DUNMAIL RAISE

Dunmail Raise is a large round cairn found in the valley between Helvellyn and Steel Fell, in the central reservation of the A591. Round cairns are mounds of stone that cover cists, burial spaces resembling modern coffins. Cists are found at both Neolithic and Bronze Age sites, but those found within round cairns are almost certainly Bronze Age.

Round cairns replaced the shared burial chambers of the Neolithic period. Progressively throughout the Bronze Age, fewer people were interred into shared burial chambers, and single cairn burials eventually became the norm. Large round cairns like Dunmail Raise may represent the earliest adoption of this tradition; a grave large enough to hold multiple bodies in Neolithic fashion, but in the round cairn style of the Bronze Age.

This is not to imply that round cairns are a more advanced monument type to those found in the Neolithic however, quite the opposite in fact. As the British population swelled during the Bronze Age, the need to construct burial monuments quickly may have contributed to the popularity of the round cairn. Neolithic builders often constructed ornate tombs for their dead, while Bronze Age round cairns, conversely, were less complex and constructed using smaller stones.

– THIRLMERE CUPS –

It is unanimously believed that Dunmail Raise was an ancient burial marker, but the question for many is – *for whom*? Despite the clear evidence that this is a prehistoric round cairn, its origins are often confused. If you read any tourist information about Dunmail Raise, it is presumably described as a tomb for 'King Dunmail', '*Cumbria's last king*.' Not only is this untrue, but little evidence suggests that King Dunmail himself is anything more than a legend. This probably originated in the eighteenth or nineteenth century, when a busy horse track passed right beside the cairn. Curious travellers or farmers likely discovered bones while quarrying the stones, birthing the folklore.

The truth is that nobody really knows who was buried here. Dunmail Raise was most likely a burial tomb containing the remains of several eminent Bronze Age people.

Author's Notes: In a small patch of woodland, to the north of Dunmail Raise, is another collection of Neolithic cup marks. Four cups are etched into a rock overlooking Thirlmere, demonstrating that people had clearly traversed over this hillside for thousands of years.

RYDAL CAIRNS

Venturing into the valley between the peaks of the Fairfield Horseshoe, beside the shores of Rydal Beck, you can find three small burial cairns. These burials, which we will refer to as the Rydal Cairns, are typical Bronze Age burial markers: raised mounds of stone that cover burial cists.

Unlike larger burial cairns, such as Dunmail Raise, the Rydal Cairns are short and flat, probably the handiwork of a smaller Bronze Age farming community. During the time they were built, the climate was wetter, and the most suitable farmland was found on sheltered hillside valleys. The fields next to Rydal Beck would have been an ideal place to farm, and so it is likely that a Bronze Age settlement once existed here.

The Rydal Cairns have yet to be excavated, and all three burials have been left undisturbed. This is rare, as during the Victorian period, a significant number of these burial markers were destroyed by overly eager antiquarians and landowners seeking building materials. But if they had been excavated, what might have been found within these cairns?

The answer is complicated. While they probably date to the Bronze Age, burial cairns changed in style repeatedly throughout the period, from large multi-burials such as Dunmail Raise, to small single burials. But put simply: the Rydal Cairns contain human remains. Depending on the date they were built, the cairns may contain either bones, human ashes or urns.

A prevalent pattern is the discovery of adults and children buried together, possibly a way for them to stay together into the afterlife. Other times, these were single burials, possibly grave markers used by chieftains or religious leaders.

Author's Notes: These are the mausoleums of people who lived more than 4,000 years ago. If not for their remote location, the Rydal Cairns probably would not have survived the onslaught of modern developments. Their survival is a testament to the importance of preservation. Which is exactly why we must pay respect to unstable cairns like these. Please do not move or walk on any of the stones – their existence can be appreciated from a distance, without the risk of causing unnecessary damage.

LOW KINGATE

This ruinous stone circle is found on the western edge of the Troutbeck Valley, nestled within a woodland adjacent to the A592. It can be accessed via a public footpath leading down from Kirkstone Pass, where you can find it opposite a disused quarry.

Low Kingate is a rare form of stone circle known as a concentric: two or more rings of stone arranged within one another. In this case, the outer circle is severely damaged and hardly noticeable, and only two stones remain visible in the inner circle. Out of approximately 250 stone circles found across England, only fifteen of them are considered concentric.

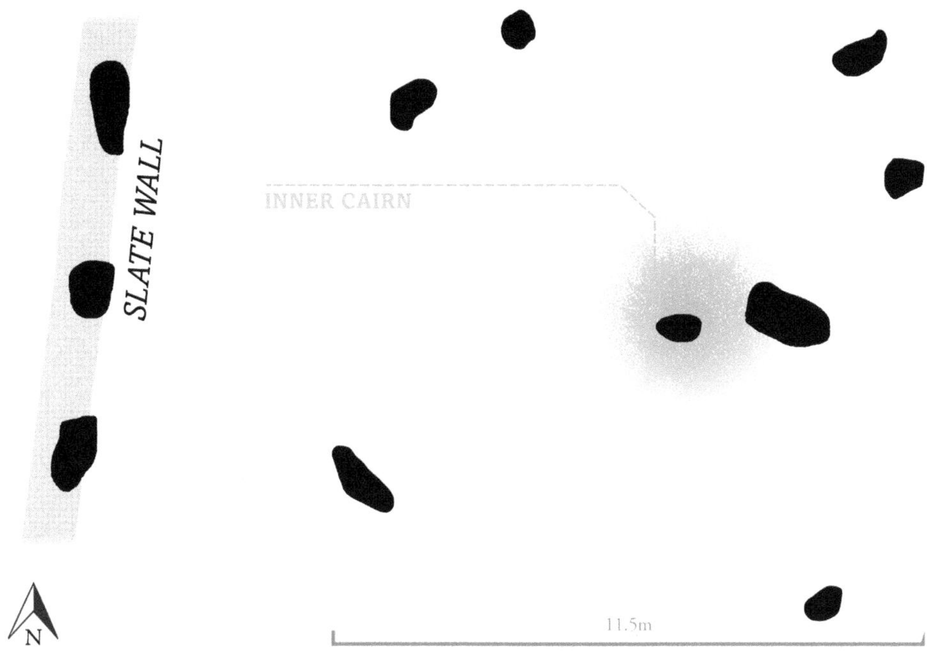

– LOW KINGATE'S VISIBLE STONES, AS SEEN FROM ABOVE –

In the nineteenth century, a burial cairn was uncovered within the centre of the inner circle. While pillaging rock from this cairn, quarry workers unearthed a stone axe head, likely from Langdale. At the time of its discovery, little was understood about the Langdale Axe Factory, and an axe's inclusion within a stone circle was seen as curious. The axe head was partly polished, which led some antiquarians to conclude that its shape was a result of water erosion. As we now understand, Neolithic craftspeople were highly skilled, and hundreds of polished axe heads can be traced back to the Lake District.

The axe head displayed signs of wear and tear, characteristic of cutting trees, indicating that it had been used before being buried. *But why was a stone axe head buried here?* By the Bronze Age, Langdale axe heads may have been cherished antiques. Its inclusion within a burial cairn was possibly to ensure that the deceased took it with them into the afterlife. The fact that the axe had been a practical tool, clearly used, suggests that it may have belonged to, and had been used by, someone who was buried here.

Concentric stone circles like Low Kingate almost always include a cairn within their centre. Comparable circles have been found to contain multiple bodies, leading some to conclude that they are simply the extravagant graves for eminent Bronze Age people.

Author's Notes: Many more prehistoric sites exist within the Troutbeck Valley. The Tongue, a small fell in the centre of the valley, has numerous round cairns built on it, and two more are found beside the shores of Trout Beck. The remains of a Bronze Age farming settlement are also situated directly opposite Low Kingate, on the western side of the Tongue.

THE NORTH LAKES

ESTIMATED DATE OF OCCUPATION

3200 BC

The North Lakes is a region renowned for its magnificent lakes and soaring fells. While generally few prehistoric monuments have survived here, the quality and age of these sites ranks them among the finest British archaeology has to offer.

The basin in which the town of Keswick sits serves as a vast junction, allowing the easiest routes between Penrith, the Irish Sea and Scotland, making it an ideal place to trade. Keswick's usefulness as a junction continues into modern times, with its tourist trade being among the most valuable in northern England. Before the tourists, however, Keswick was renowned for the trade in metals and stone, as far back as ancient and prehistoric times. A Neolithic settlement known as 'Mossgarth' is situated at the north end of Derwent Water, which was found to contain the highest concentration of Langdale axes in the Lake District. This discovery may suggest that Keswick was an area where axe heads were honed, polished, and traded, and for this reason, several researchers have linked the stone circles at Keswick to the Langdale Axe Factory.

It is no surprise, then, that many of Cumbria's most impressive prehistoric monuments are found at either end of the Threlkeld Valley, which stretches 15 miles between Keswick and Penrith. This route would have allowed easy transit between eastern and western Cumbria and is the fastest route between the Langdale Axe Factory and Scotland.

When antiquarian William Stukeley visited the North Lakes in 1725, he described numerous large stone circles in the area. No evidence remains of these circles, and today his accounts are mostly discredited. One thing is clear, however – the North Lakes is an incredibly valuable ancient landscape, and a must-visit region for anyone interested in the field of archaeology.

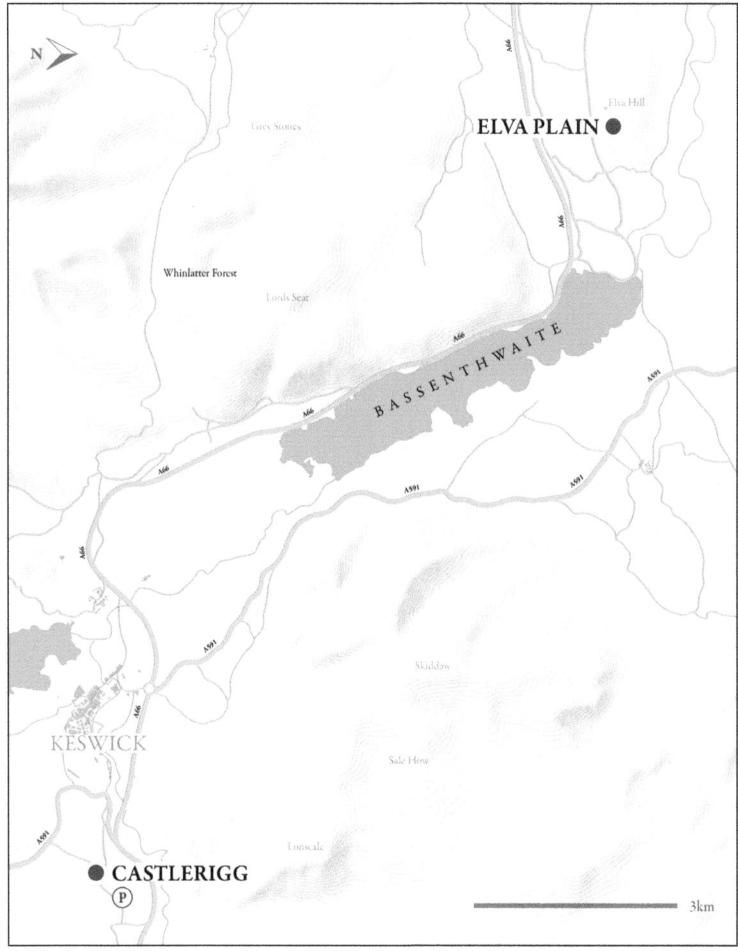

– THE NORTH LAKES –

CASTLERIGG

Castlerigg is the most visited prehistoric monument in Cumbria, and for good reason. Among the oldest stone circles in Britain, dated to an estimated 3200 BC, Castlerigg may be well over 1,200 years older than the Pyramids of Giza.

If you can find a quiet day, when you have the circle all to yourself, Castlerigg is a truly breathtaking site. Its position, on a small hill near Keswick, one of the busiest tourist towns in the Lake District, is both a positive and a negative for anyone visiting. While you have easy access to one of the most impressive stone circles in England (*and a nearby ice-cream van*), you are unlikely to get it all to yourself unless you visit out of season or early in the morning. The best time of year to enjoy Castlerigg is January to May, when you can get the clearest views with fewer visitors. It is also recommended that you head here late at night to do some star gazing; the night sky will never look better. Being able to pace around at your own leisure and admire the way the stones frame the night sky is an experience you won't soon forget.

GREEN ARROW: DIAMOND CARVING
BLUE: INNER CHAMBER
RED: PORTAL STONES

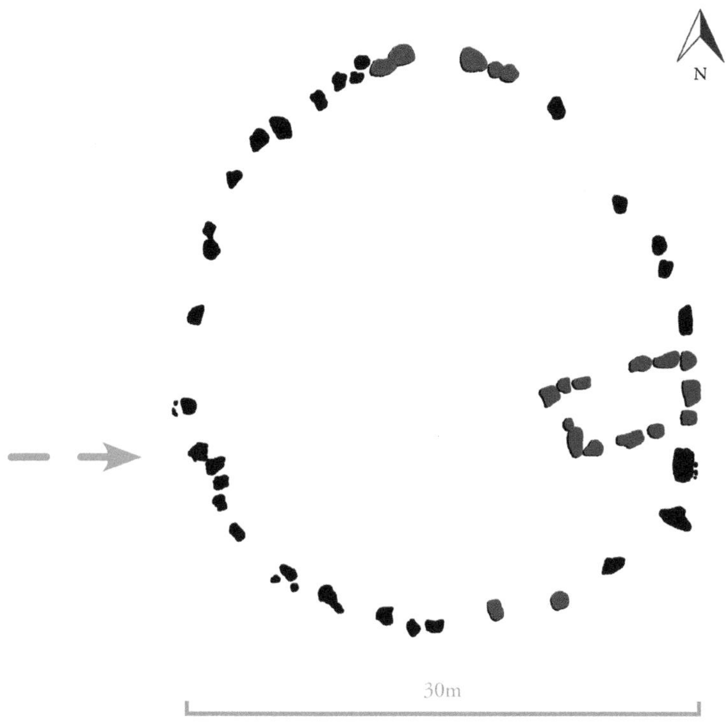

– CASTLERIGG FROM ABOVE –

Thirty-eight large boulders are arranged in an egg-shaped configuration. On its eastern side is a rectangular enclosure, an unusual feature unique to Castlerigg. The purpose of the enclosure is a mystery, and the countless theories on its uses remain unproven. What researchers do understand, however, is that this enclosure was likely not a grave, as numerous excavations have failed to find any human remains within it. At the northern edge of the circle is a well-defined gap, flanked by two tall stones, possibly an intentionally aligned entranceway. To the south is a second gap that opens the circle outwards towards the valley, presenting one of the most iconic views of the Lake District. Whether this was intended or simply a happy accident is not known, but it makes for some majestic photography.

A lone stone found near the wall to the south-west of the circle was erected by a farmer in the early twentieth century. All evidence suggests that this outlying stone was originally buried, so its authenticity as an original feature is not known. It is often theorised that outlying stones were used like the sights on a rifle, targeting where the solstice sun rises or sets. This may have been the case here, or this stone may have no connection to Castlerigg at all. There really is no way to know.

Castlerigg is truly a time capsule from the Neolithic, almost perfectly preserved, and only shy of four stones. Perhaps one reason why it has remained so well maintained is its isolation. While sites of a similar age have been scarred by modern developments, Castlerigg has stayed secluded on a remote hilltop for over 5,000 years. When viewed in this context Castlerigg is, conceivably, one of the purest examples of a stone circle in Britain. Despite the importance of Castlerigg to our understanding of Britain's historical timeline, no modern excavations have been undertaken here. One of the more relevant questions that we can ask concerns its location:

Why is one of the oldest stone circles in Britain here?

People regularly speculate about the sun setting behind arbitrary stones in the circle, but this is unprovable and perhaps nonsensical. Of course, every point around a circle aligns to something. So, as we have a near perfectly preserved stone circle to study, analysing it as it stands might be the best course. A single entranceway was created using two large portal stones to the north, and a rectangular enclosure stands to the east. Larger stones are scattered evenly throughout the circle which help to form Castlerigg's shape, giving it a nicely balanced appearance. Aside from the dubious theory about the outlying stone, no single element definitively points towards the solstice sun, so maybe we need to think more practically. Perhaps Castlerigg is an enclosure with a more nuanced story to tell …

Antiquarian excavations in the eighteenth century unearthed three Langdale axe heads from within Castlerigg. Because of this, and the various Langdale axes discovered at Mossgarth, several researchers (including famed archaeologist

– CASTLERIGG'S INNER ENCLOSURE, WINTER –

Aubrey Burl) theorised that Castlerigg may have been connected to the axe trade. This theory would suggest that Castlerigg was used as a trading hub of sorts, or a religious centre inside which pilgrims left offerings. If we assume this scenario is plausible, we can infer that the fells surrounding Castlerigg may have represented the Langdale Pikes and its numerous quarries. Its position at the centre of such an awe-inspiring valley may have served a purpose like murals on the side of a church, the mountains being a symbolic reference to the Langdale Axe Factory. This is, of course, just one theory.

Four burial cairns are found within the northern half of the circle, two of which have visible ditches surrounding them. We can only speculate why burials took place within Castlerigg, but it is doubtful the cairns are original features. These were probably later additions, made during the Bronze Age, using Castlerigg's splendour as a means of aggrandising otherwise unremarkable burials. Castlerigg's original purpose was presumably long forgotten (or ignored) by this point in prehistory, and so Bronze Age activity here is puzzling. It could be reasoned that these stones still held spiritual importance long into the Bronze Age, but in what context remains a mystery.

Another later addition may be the only surviving carving at Castlerigg: a small diamond motif etched onto the side of a fallen stone at the western edge of the circle. While this may have been the work of prehistoric hands, its legitimacy is questionable. Analysis of the carving suggests it was created using metal tools, evidence that it was added after the Bronze Age. However, diamond motifs like this can be contemporary with the Neolithic, with the stones of Newgrange in Ireland being good examples.

– THE DIAMOND CARVING –

Author's Notes: It needs to be said with absolute clarity, as is true for most Neolithic stone circles in Britain, the function of Castlerigg essentially remains a mystery. It is just one of many Neolithic monuments that demonstrate how limited our understanding of the period truly is. Predictably, it is only natural that speculation will fill the void when there are gaps in the research.

Thanks to attention-grabbing tourist information, speculation is often presented as indisputable fact, and the public misses the remarkable mystery that Castlerigg presents. Here is a site that is not only aesthetically striking, but the questions it begs to have answered are among the most important in British archaeology. Simple explanations are perhaps all too naive, and the acceptance of our collective ignorance on the topic is too crushing for some to accept.

That is not to say we should shy away from speculation; in fact, speculating is exactly what we should be doing when confronted with a site like Castlerigg. But speculation is not necessarily based in fact. It is only through the tireless work of universities, councils and history societies that we can get closer to the real answers.

ELVA PLAIN

Elva Plain is a large stone circle north of Bassenthwaite Lake, on the aptly named Elva Hill. It is easily accessed via a boggy footpath that leads up the hill from the nearby road.

Comparisons to Castlerigg are common, largely due to its similar width and mountain vistas. On a decent day you can expect some of the best views of Grisedale Pike and Skiddaw. If we are witnessing the work of a people who

– ELVA PLAIN STONE CIRCLE –

venerated their surrounding landscapes, then this would undoubtedly be consecrated ground. Aside from the views, however, Elva Plain is a far less inspiring circle than Castlerigg, only retaining half of its original stone count. Those that remain are either fallen or small. In total, only fifteen out of an estimated thirty stones remain.

While its current level of preservation leaves a lot to be decoded, the circle's size is perhaps its most revealing aspect. Wide stone circles like Elva Plain, created using large boulders, typically date to the Neolithic or Early Bronze

– ELVA PLAIN FROM ABOVE –

Age periods. These early stone circles are believed to have enclosed religious gatherings, not unlike a modern church or mosque. Like those modern counterparts, it is possible that this circle served many different functions during use, from simple worship to funeral ceremonies.

Antiquarians in the nineteenth century reported a now lost outlying stone to the south-west, which may have served the purpose of aligning the circle towards the winter solstice sunset. Unfortunately, the stone is now lost, and was likely smashed to make room for ploughing in the nineteenth century. The sun falling behind this outlying stone might have been used to signal the setting of the winter solstice sun, an indication of the year's end and the cold winter to come.

Author's Notes: It is often speculated that Elva Plain was an area to trade Langdale axes. During research, I have found no credible source for this (other than a tenuous link between the name 'Elva' and 'elfshot', meaning axe head). No Langdale axe heads have ever been found at the site. Without modern excavations, I would rather not make assumptions.

BLEABERRY HAWS

ESTIMATED DATE OF OCCUPATION

Middle Bronze Age (est. 1500 BC)

On a moorland fell under the shadow of Coniston Old Man sits a collection of Bronze Age settlements, cairns and stone circles. It is a region often neglected by sightseers, possibly in favour of the more glamorous fells to the north. For this reason, the countless monuments that exist under Coniston Old Man have been left little explored.

The most wonderfully preserved of these sites can be found clustered around a small hill called Bleaberry Haws. Five Bronze Age ruins have been identified on this hill, as well as an unexcavated circular enclosure to the east. The area is rather inaccessible, but an arduous trek from Torver allows access to the moor. A single footpath snakes north towards an abandoned mine, and a wet walk through a bog is required to appreciate these fine ruins.

The monuments here are generally smaller than in other regions of Cumbria and appear like miniaturised versions of larger examples found across the county. It is likely then, that this area was home to several smaller Bronze Age communities, who desired to build stone monuments but lacked the manpower to do so on the grand scale seen elsewhere.

As with the cairns at Rydal, you must factor in survivor bias when trying to understand the ancient people who lived here. The location of these monuments, on a secluded hilltop, should not necessarily suggest that this was a popular place to build during the Bronze Age. Prehistoric settlements in the most obvious areas, on low ground for instance, were destroyed to make way for our modern towns and villages long ago. Therefore, it is only examples built in remote areas like this that have survived into the modern day.

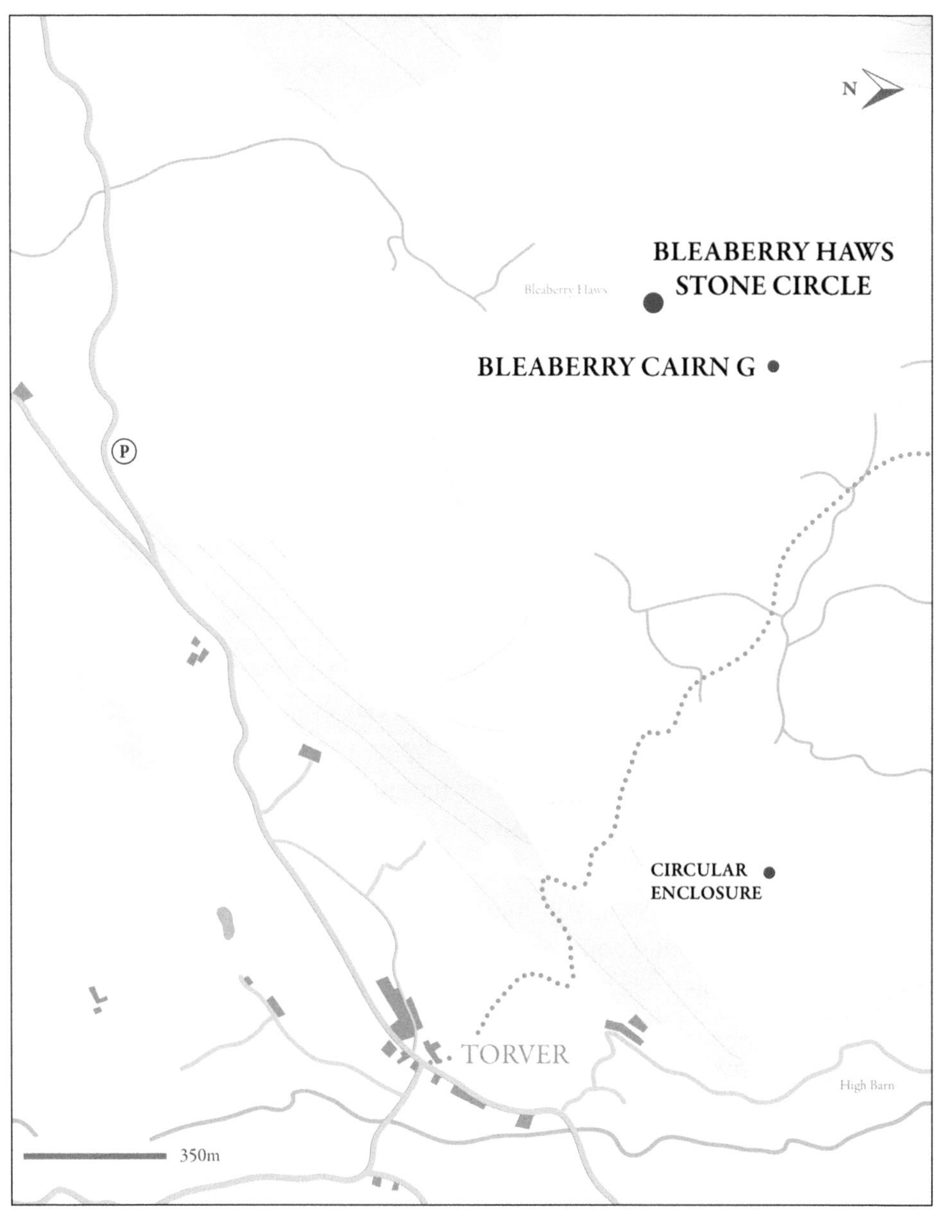
N
BLEABERRY HAWS
STONE CIRCLE
Bleaberry Haws
BLEABERRY CAIRN G
P
CIRCULAR
ENCLOSURE
TORVER
High Barn
350m

BLEABERRY HAWS STONE CIRCLE

Bleaberry Haws Stone Circle can be found on the brow of a hill overlooking the nearby Bursting Stone Quarry. Finding it can be a challenge, as for most of the year its small stones are obscured by tall grass.

While this is certainly a circle, created using stones, this is not a stone circle by any traditional definition. It is tiny, comprising only seven small stones. The inner area of the circle is clearly raised, giving the circle a crown-like appearance. These details would usually imply that a circle is either a burial monument or building foundation.

During an 1887 excavation, a neat pavement of cobblestones was discovered beneath the circle's centre, laid in only a single layer and containing no human remains. The antiquarian leading the dig, H. S. Cowper, believed that this might be a hut circle, the surviving stone base of a round house. The structure's walls and roof have rotted away, leaving only the retaining stones.

Hut circles were common throughout the Bronze Age, but especially during the mid to late period (1500 BC–700 BC). These houses were similarly shaped to a tipi tent, with a large thatched roof that extended over the retaining walls. A stone base would have ensured that any damage to the roof could have easily been replaced without ripping out the foundations.

Bleaberry Haws Stone Circle is only a small example of such a building, but bigger, better-preserved examples are found in Devon. Bleaberry Haws was presumably once littered with small wooden huts. Not unlike manor houses, or Roman villas, the stone-based huts here may have belonged to higher-status members of the community. Of course, the social structure of the Bronze Age is not easily understood, and it is not known exactly who would have constituted high status.

It is somewhat puzzling why only a single stone-based round house was built on Bleaberry Haws. In other areas of Britain, hut circles are commonly found clustered together, or in walled settlements. While there are no such clusters found on Bleaberry Haws, there is a nearby structure that could suggest the existence of a settlement. Across the moor, at Banishead Quarry, you can find a wide enclosure known as The Rigg. Despite being heavily damaged, some believe this enclosure to have once been a walled settlement.

BLEABERRY CAIRNS

Four small burial cairns surround Bleaberry Haws. They are just one cluster of cairns among many found on the moor below Coniston Old Man.

Nineteenth century excavations unearthed urns and tools from inside the cairns. This strongly suggests that the Bleaberry Cairns were created during the Bronze Age, since urns tend to appear in the archaeological record from around 2500 BC onwards. While it is easy to mistakenly assume that people were intentionally going out of their way to build cairns in remote areas, it is now known that they probably lived close by. As was the case at Rydal, these cairns were likely created by a small Bronze Age farming community, utilising the moorland for agriculture.

Prehistoric Britons left no written records of their social structure, and only a few clues have arisen to help us understand who was buried within cairns like these. For this reason, it is perhaps best to first explain *why* cairn burials took place. Archaeologists can only speculate on why people were buried here, but

– THE ROUND CAIRN TO THE NORTH OF THE HILL, 'BLEABERRY G' –

several theories about the purpose of small cairns like these have been presented:

1. Only high-status members of Bronze Age society would have received cairn burials.

2. Cairn burials were shared, serving to hold the remains of people from the surrounding communities, much like a modern-day graveyard.

3. Burial rituals evolved throughout the Bronze Age, and cairns designed to hold single burials were later reused as the population swelled.

Theory number two is probably correct in this case. The cairn's small scale and rough designs suggest that they were simple, utilitarian sites designed to cover multiple urns.

But if they were 'simply utilitarian', why build them on a hill?

People of the Bronze Age presumably chose to be buried amid magnificent scenery, as we continue to do today. And as evidenced by the hundreds of similar monuments found on the coast, Bleaberry Haws is only the tip of the iceberg.

OTHER SITES IN THE CENTRAL LAKE DISTRICT

While all prehistoric sites are valuable, not all have had the luxury of in-depth investigations. These are the sites that have eluded comprehensive study, since they are either too damaged, too small or simply lacking excavation or survey.

THE RUSLAND MENHIR

The Rusland Menhir is a lonely egg-shaped menhir, perched on the top of a low hill by a small river. It can be viewed from the nearby Rusland Moss Nature Reserve.

A feature directly beneath the stone looks like an unexcavated cairn made of the same quartzite stones, and so it is likely that the Rusland Menhir is a grandiose burial capstone, although the remote location is an unusual choice for such a structure. More often than not, these monuments are not found alone.

THE RIGG

Not far north-east of Bleaberry Haws is Banishead Quarry, a large abandoned slate mine. Heading from here towards Coniston Old Man you will encounter The Rigg Enclosure.

There has been little research performed on this structure, although it appears to be a half ring of stones set into a D shape. Over half of the site was destroyed by the construction of the path; therefore discerning the function of The Rigg is almost impossible at this point.

BANNISIDE CIRCLE

Banniside Circle is another curious monument to the north-east of Bleaberry Haws. It isn't a particularly conspicuous monument, being just a simple ring of cobblestones. Despite this, W. G. Collingwood, President of the Cumberland and Westmorland Antiquarian Society, excavated the site in 1901. The dig uncovered a trove of Bronze Age artifacts from within the circle's centre. Among the items uncovered were urns, well-preserved pottery specimens, jewellery beads and stone tools. After almost completely excavating the cairn and restoring its edges, Collingwood concluded that Banniside Circle was a cremation cemetery, a circle used to enclose cremations during the Bronze Age.

FOUR STONES HILL

The not-so-aptly named Four Stones Hill can be found to the north of Haweswater. This hillside is home to several Bronze Age constructions, hut enclosures, round cairns and, most notably, *two* standing stones. Both stones are around 4ft in height and appear to be aligned to the winter solstice sunrise and, conversely, the summer solstice sunset.

PATTERDALE ROCK ART

The Patterdale Rock Art, a collection of cup-marked rocks similar to those at Grasmere, is found just north of Kirkstone Pass, near the small village of Bridgend. This is an easy site to find, and you can access it via a footpath running parallel to the main road.

– HARTSOP HALL ROUND CAIRN –

HARTSOP HALL ROUND CAIRN

Despite being relatively unknown, Hartsop Hall Round Cairn is one of the more charming tumuli in the Lake District. Located at the tail end of Kirkstone Pass, it can be found next to a Roman settlement known as Dovedale. It is large, around 20m in diameter, and covered with earth.

A small semi-circle of megaliths arcs across its top, and a long flat capstone covers a ransacked cist. There has been little study of the monument, but it is worth a visit, if only to appreciate the nearby Roman ruins.

Some have argued that the Dovedale settlement is the converted remains of a henge monument, which are covered in detail in Chapter 5. If true, then this is a rare place indeed.

HIGH TOVE RING CAIRN

This seldom visited ring of stones lies on a hillside overlooking Borrowdale, near the peak of High Tove. Fifteen stones appear to sit in an oval arrangement on plateaued ground. Although its name implies that it is a ring cairn, there is little known about its form, as most of the monument remains buried under the ground.

CHAPTER 2

THE IRISH SEA

People first travelled to Cumbria around 10,000 BC, spreading north through Morecambe Bay, eventually landing on the fertile Cumbrian coast. It was here, during the Mesolithic period, that people began to develop their affinity for stonework.

Before the invention of the polished stone axe in the Neolithic period, tools were predominantly created using flint. This sharp stone is naturally found along pebble beaches, which are common in Cumbria. The Cumbrian coast was home to many flint-knapping sites in the Neolithic period. Evidence for this is often found in the form of flint tool-bits buried alongside burials. Although flint was used throughout the Stone Age, some artifacts have a greater association with the Neolithic. Microliths, for example, were small tool-bits used for cutting and scraping.

The Cumbrian coast is home to several uniquely small stone circles, which are almost always found in areas allowing both sea and mountain views. Their position may represent another example of survivor bias. As is seen repeatedly across Europe, prehistoric sites have survived especially well on moorland tracts. Many untouched moors overlook the Irish Sea. Therefore, hundreds of smaller burial monuments, which would otherwise have been destroyed long ago, have survived. For this reason, Bronze Age sites, commonly found on upland moors, are especially numerous in this region.

Between the Vikings and the Victorians, Cumbria's coastline has changed to accommodate both invasions and technological innovations. Today, this is easily Cumbria's most developed region, where you can always find yourself a place to rest and recharge. From Workington to Barrow-in-Furness, the A595 enables fast travel up and down the coast.

BURNMOOR

ESTIMATED DATE OF OCCUPATION

Early / Middle Bronze Age

One of the most comprehensive collections of prehistoric burial monuments in England, Burnmoor is a little-known archaeological paradise. Occupying a moorland plateau below the imposing peak of Scafell Pike, this is a prehistoric burial ground on a scale unlike anywhere else in Cumbria. Burnmoor boasts up to 400 prehistoric cairns and five stone circles; for an enthusiast in British prehistory it is certainly a sight to behold.

It is not clear why people of the Bronze Age would make the ascent to this boggy moor, but farming is likely a good guess. Britain was wetter and warmer during the Early Bronze Age, and the most arable farmland was found on sheltered moorland. Burnmoor's large flat surface area would have made it a perfect place to farm, and its situation under Scafell Pike and the Axe Factory was undoubtedly a plus. Most of the cairns on the moor are clearance cairns, long piles of stone that were simply moved aside to make room for farmland. Further evidence for heavy farming can be seen in the lynchets to the north-east of the moor: terraced farms dating to the Bronze Age. Not unlike Asian rice paddies, or the stepped sides of Machu Picchu, British lynchets made the best of the cooler climate at higher altitudes to grow crops.

Nevertheless, a short time spent walking the various trails across Burnmoor will demonstrate why this landscape was so attractive. From one end to the other you can see some of the most superb views that England has to offer. Hardknott and its various tarns are visible to the east, and the Irish Sea to the south. Of course, settling your community so close to both the Axe Factory and the Irish Sea was certainly of strategic benefit for a sea-faring people.

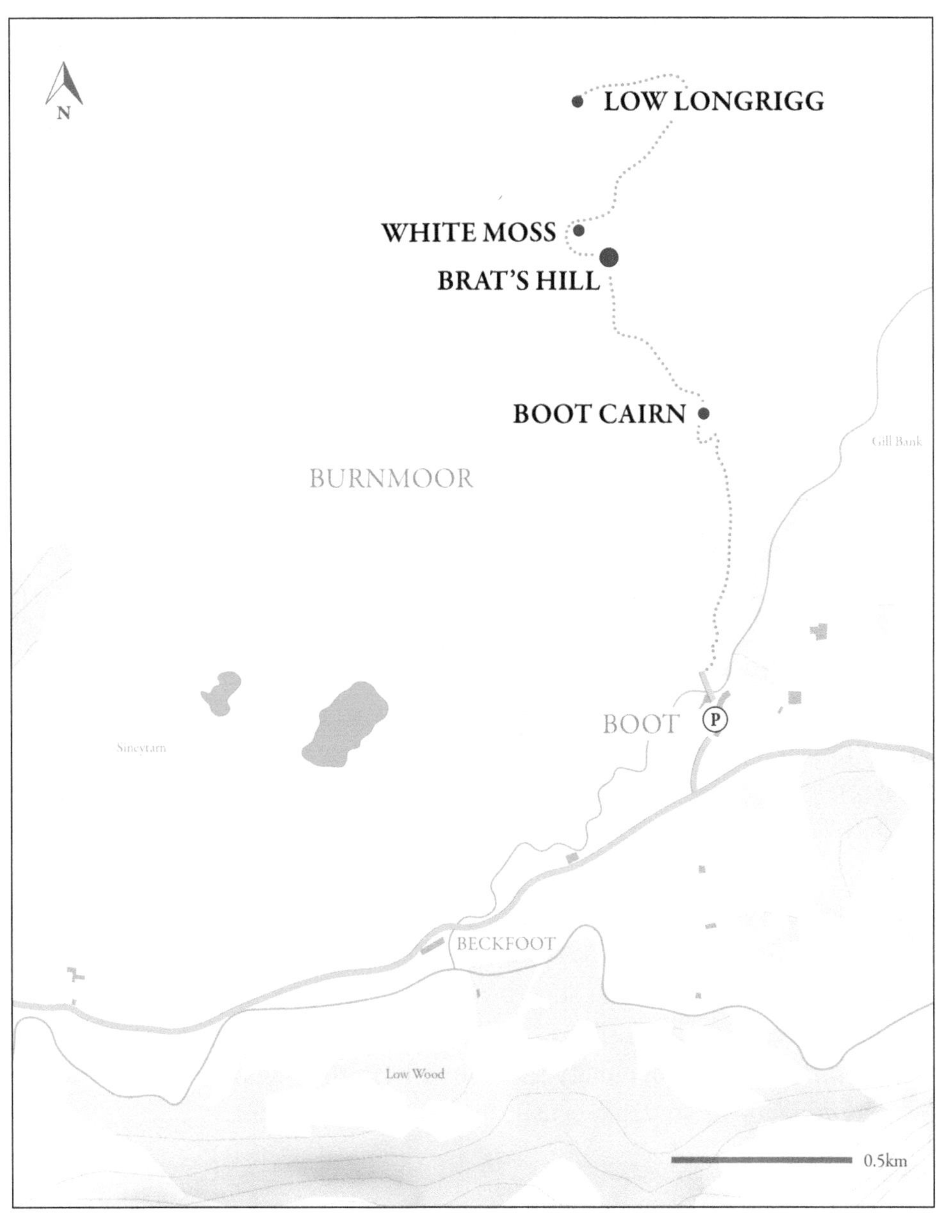

BRAT'S HILL

Brat's Hill Stone Circle is located at the brow of the moor. It is the largest stone circle found on Burnmoor, and the third widest in Cumbria. A craggy outcrop stands to the immediate south of the circle, a feature that is far more prominent than the circle itself. Standing on this crag allows for the grandest views over the monuments on Burnmoor, framing Brat's Hill in the foreground between Great How and Scafell Pike.

Its most distinctive feature is a collection of cairns clustered around the south-west quadrant of the circle. An excavation in 1872 unearthed partially cremated bones and urn fragments from within the cairns. These bones had been buried in a fashion typical of the Early Bronze Age and have since been dated to approximately 2500 BC.

The position of the cairns indicates that the north-east quadrant of the circle was kept clear by design. Some archaeologists have suggested that this was to align people towards the south-west, pointing funeral spectators towards the winter solstice sunset as bodies were interred inside the cairns. Assuming that people were buried soon after death, there is one obvious flaw in this theory: people probably didn't plan their deaths to coincide with the winter solstice. Instead, it could be argued that the cairns were positioned this way for later ceremonies, maybe to honour those buried within the cairns later in the year.

A rectangular enclosure, not unlike the one found at Castlerigg, was mentioned by architect Dr. James Fergusson in 1872. He noted:

– BRAT'S HILL'S LARGEST STONE –

– BRAT'S HILL FROM ABOVE –
(the blue representing the inner burial cairns)

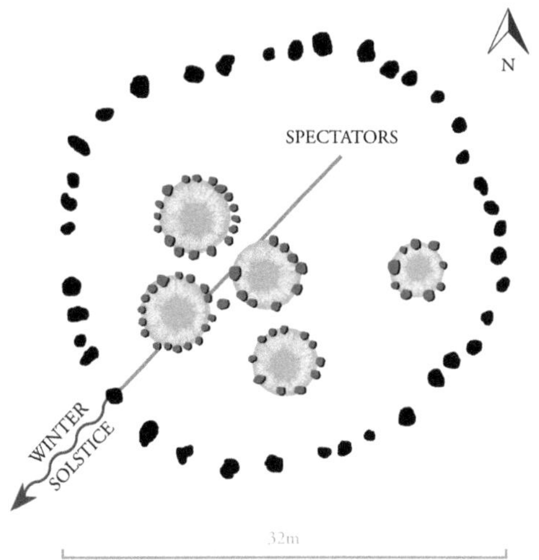

A niche or square enclosure on one side of the inner circle contains a cairn 25ft in diameter, and within the circle are four others, irregularly spaced, and measuring 21 to 25ft in diameter, each like the circle itself, surrounded by fourteen stones.

If his account is to be believed, a square enclosure of stones was removed from Brat's Hill at some point during the nineteenth century. No evidence of this has ever been found, however, and it is believed that his description was either a misidentification or fabrication.

Unfortunately for those envisioning robed rituals and animal sacrifices, Brat's Hill was probably not a religious enclosure in the classical sense. The stones are small and roughly sprawled into a circle, seemingly without care for aesthetic design. Hardly the place to worship a god. With a litany of similar sites available for us to compare it to, we can deduce that this was not an enclosure used for celebrations or feasts (like Castlerigg or Elva Plain, for instance).

Instead, working from circumstantial evidence, we can infer that Brat's Hill Stone Circle was created to be used as a simple burial enclosure. Many similar enclosures can be found on moorlands across Cumbria, such as Banniside Circle to the east of Bleaberry Haws. Brat's Hill was possibly a variant of such an enclosure, allowing multiple generations of an Early Bronze Age community to be buried as a group. In this sense, Brat's Hill could be considered a prehistoric family plot, or graveyard.

There remains the question of the monument's original intent. Was this a converted religious enclosure? Do the graves belong to a single family? How many generations of the community were buried here? No theory gives good reason to point in any direction with confidence, and in this situation the best we can do is speculate. The evidence for Brat's Hill being a burial monument is strong (the presence of buried bones for instance), and so it may be best to first work out who was buried here. Here are just four theories:

1. Brat's Hill was a monument created to hold the bodies of chieftains or religious leaders over the course of generations, not unlike Westminster Abbey.

2. Brat's Hill was used communally; a place a farming community used to bury their dead throughout the Bronze Age, like a modern graveyard.

3. Brat's Hill was comparable to a family mausoleum, allowing multiple generations to remain buried together.

4. Brat's Hill was a stone circle used for ritual ceremonies during the Neolithic/Early Bronze Age. The cairns were added much later in the Bronze Age by people who had lost the meaning of the circle's original religious significance.

Theory number four is perhaps the most fascinating, as it would imply the circle predates the burial cairns by a long stretch of time. Regrettably, there is no way to know for sure if this was the case, as the burial cairns may have been added at any point throughout the Bronze Age. Working purely from the simplest explanation, however, we can assume that theory number one is the case, as there are only five cairns, implying the circle saw only a limited use.

WHITE MOSS

The two White Moss Stone Circles were erected directly opposite Brat's Hill. These are wonderful examples of a common stone circle variety known as burial circles: Bronze Age burial markers surrounded by a small stone circle.

The White Moss circles are thought to have been used for multiple purposes throughout the Bronze Age, both in preparing and burying the dead. They may have been places where bodies were cremated before being interred into nearby burial cairns, and possibly an area for burying renowned individuals. Interconnected funerary sites like these are typical of the Early Bronze Age and were likely created by closely settled farming communities during that period.

Author's Notes: Despite missing some stones, it appears these two circles were once near perfectly elliptical and so fail to demonstrate any solstice alignments. They may, however, have been constructed to align on a grander scale. Standing in the middle of the White Moss north-east circle, you will face the sunrise of the winter solstice when gazing towards Brat's Hill to the south-east.

– WHITE MOSS NORTH-EAST –

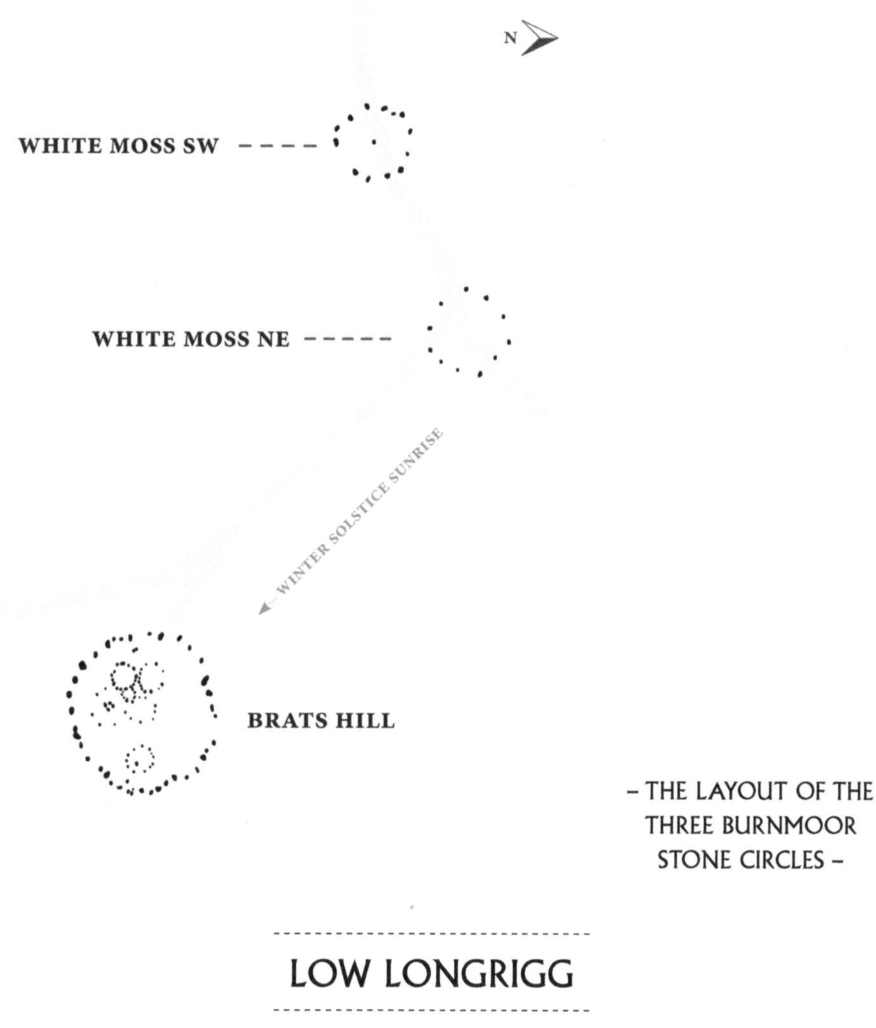

– THE LAYOUT OF THE THREE BURNMOOR STONE CIRCLES –

LOW LONGRIGG

The Low Longrigg Stone Circles are found north of Brat's Hill. They were probably burial markers, much like the other monuments on Burnmoor.

There has been confusion over the years as to exactly where these circles are located, and their plotting on historical maps has varied. This is most likely because both circles are unimpressive in comparison to White Moss, and therefore less time was given to their charting. The north circle is the widest of the two and contains the largest cairn, but the south circle is smaller with larger stones.

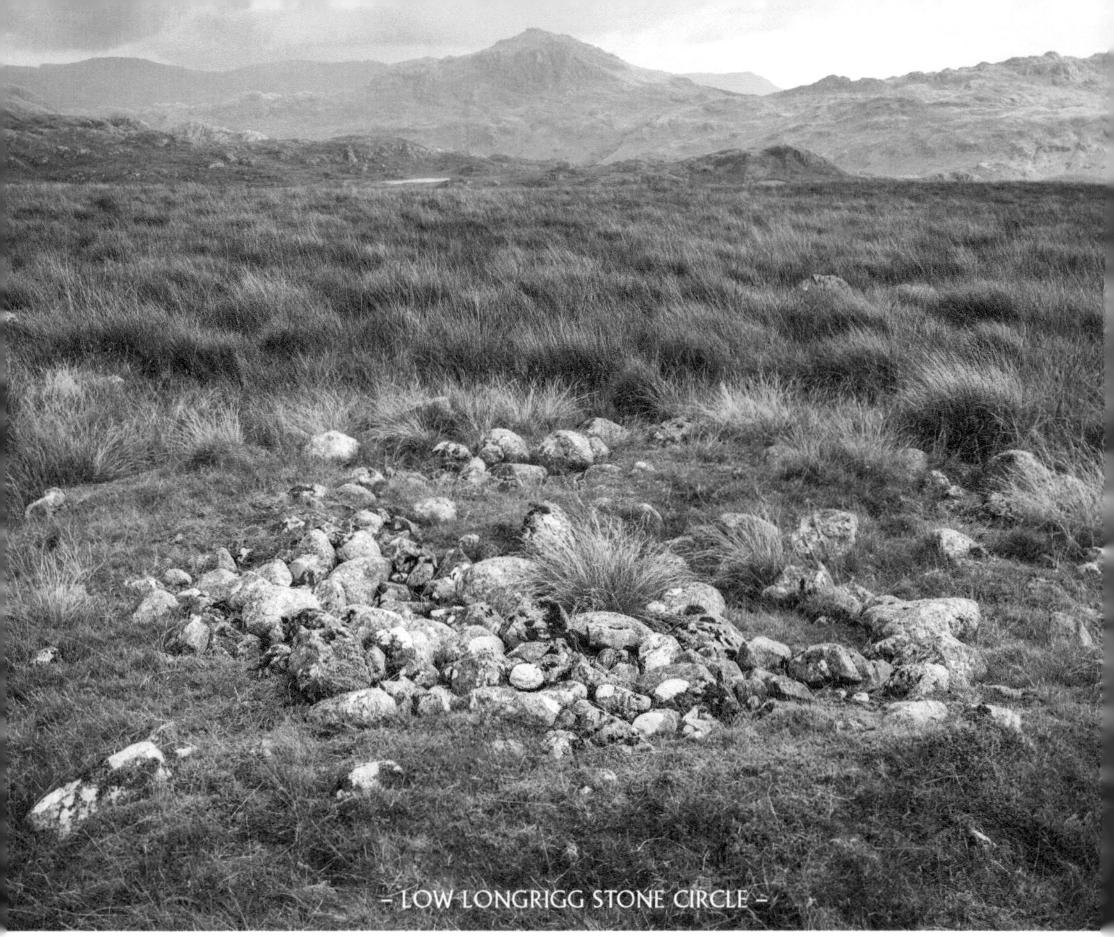

– LOW LONGRIGG STONE CIRCLE –

- LOW LONGRIGG NORTH -
- WHITE MOSS NORTHEAST -
N
- LOW LONGRIGG SOUTH -
- WHITE MOSS SOUTHWEST -

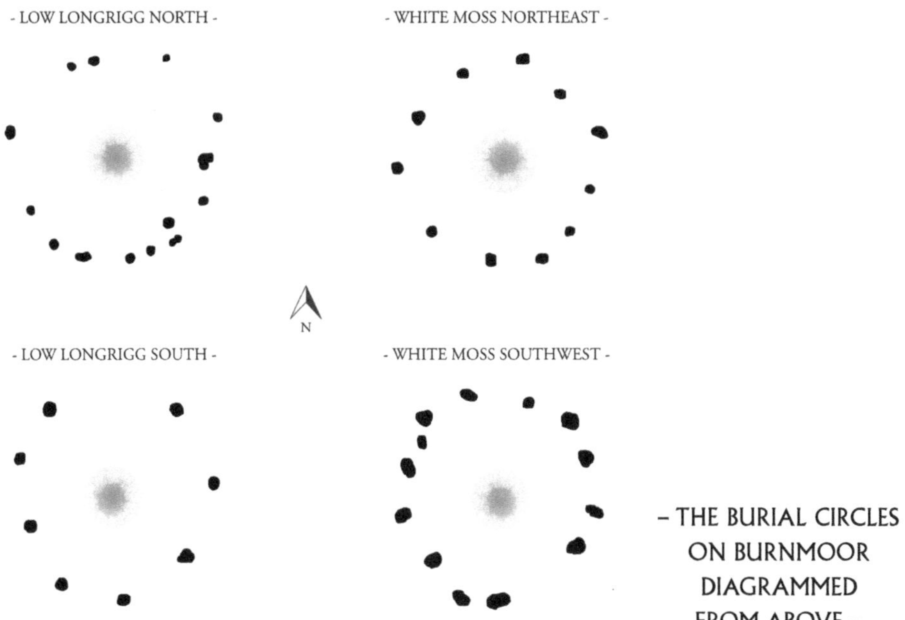

– THE BURIAL CIRCLES ON BURNMOOR DIAGRAMMED FROM ABOVE –

They were made with less bravado than the stone circles of Brat's Hill and White Moss, and their positioning further to the north suggests that they might have been built during a different period, likely later. It appears as if these circles put more importance on the size of their inner cairn. The cairn's shape and scale are similar to traditional round cairns, such as those at Bleaberry Haws, indicating that they may have been built during the Middle Bronze Age.

BOOT KERB CAIRN

Boot Kerb Cairn is just one of an estimated 400 cairns scattered adjacent to the paths across Burnmoor. It is situated between several peat huts on the way up the moor from Boot. Despite its proximity to these industrial buildings, the cairn has remained remarkably well preserved.

Kerb stones are often found surrounding cairns (such as at Low Kingate), which serve as a boundary around the cairn to keep it neatly in place, not unlike the raised crust of a pie. Kerb cairns, on the other hand, are their own variety of monument – easily identified by their obvious kerb stones. Bodies were interred within these little pie-shaped cairns during the Early Bronze Age.

Boot Kerb Cairn is the largest example of the uniquely small and flat kerb cairns found on Burnmoor. Several have been excavated, revealing burial cists within their centres. The Boot Kerb Cairn does not appear to have been disturbed, so it likely still contains the bones or cremated remains of whoever was buried there.

– BOOT KERB CAIRN –

THE FURNESS PENINSULA

ESTIMATED DATE OF OCCUPATION

Early / Middle Bronze Age

The Furness Peninsula is a 12-mile stretch of coastal land, which extends between the River Levens and Barrow-in-Furness. It is a region known for its coastal wildlife, sweeping sea views and the development of Britain's nuclear submarines. Historically part of Lancashire, the monuments found here may also reflect the work of a different culture.

Despite the peninsula being rather urbanised, it has several rural areas that are home to remarkably well-preserved prehistoric sites. Archaeological digs on Walney Island, for instance, have produced particularly impressive Neolithic pottery and jewellery artifacts – a rarity in Cumbria. A multitude of flint tools have also been discovered along the coast of Morecambe Bay, indicating a long span of settlement during the Neolithic period. Excavations have discovered that Langdale axe heads were commonly taken to this region. Over half of all Langdale stone axes discovered in Cumbria were unearthed in Furness: further evidence for an overseas trade network of these precious tools.

Most of the prehistoric sites are grouped around Great Urswick, a pretty little village with a long and varied history. The most prominent span of settlement in the area seems to have been the Early Bronze Age. During this period, several large megalithic monuments were constructed, the majority of which appear to be related to burials.

The monuments we will be covering in this area are rarely found in northern England. They may have been created by people from either Ireland or Wales, conceivably reflecting the work of a migratory culture from across the sea. It is thought the area could have been a centre for trade, possibly for the purpose of trading Langdale axes along the coast, moving items between Cumbria, Ireland, Wales and Cornwall.

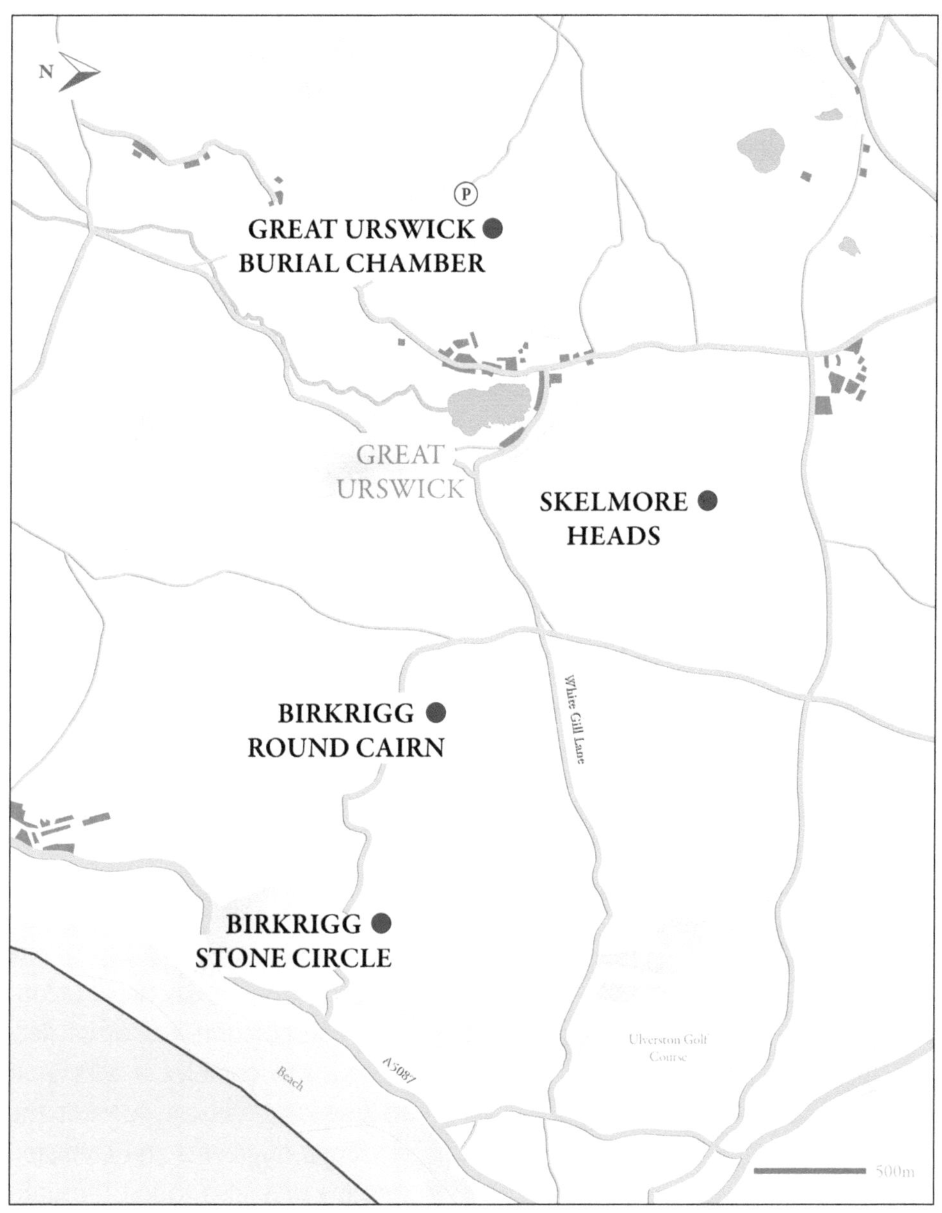
N
P
GREAT URSWICK
BURIAL CHAMBER
GREAT
URSWICK
SKELMORE
HEADS
White Gill Lane
BIRKRIGG
ROUND CAIRN
BIRKRIGG
STONE CIRCLE
Beach
A5087
Ulverston Golf
Course
500m

BIRKRIGG STONE CIRCLE

Also known by its old name Druids Temple, Birkrigg is one of the best-known concentric stone circles in England. Its stones are often used as a rest stop for those visiting Birkrigg Common, making a quiet trip to the stones somewhat difficult. If you want to experience the circle during a less busy period, the best time to visit is during winter.

Birkrigg is a double ring of stones made up of fifteen limestone megaliths around its outer ring and ten in its centre. The inner circle is the most easily visible section of Birkrigg, as the outer stones are often obscured by a dense layer of bracken. Despite this, Birkrigg is possibly the clearest example of a concentric stone circle in Cumbria. Like other concentric circles, such as Low Kingate near Grasmere, Birkrigg Stone Circle is thought to have been a monument used during funerals in the Bronze Age.

Early excavations in 1911 found an urn buried upside down within the centre of the circle, decorated in a style unique to the Early Bronze Age. While it may seem strange today, Bronze Age urns were almost always buried upside down, with their openings facing towards the earth. The top of the urn (what we today would consider the bottom), was often decorated with complex motifs, as if to present a message towards the sky. Bone fragments and cremated remains were also found throughout the circle's inner area at various depths, suggesting that bodies were cremated within the circle.

– BIRKRIGG STONE CIRCLE DIAGRAMMED FROM ABOVE –

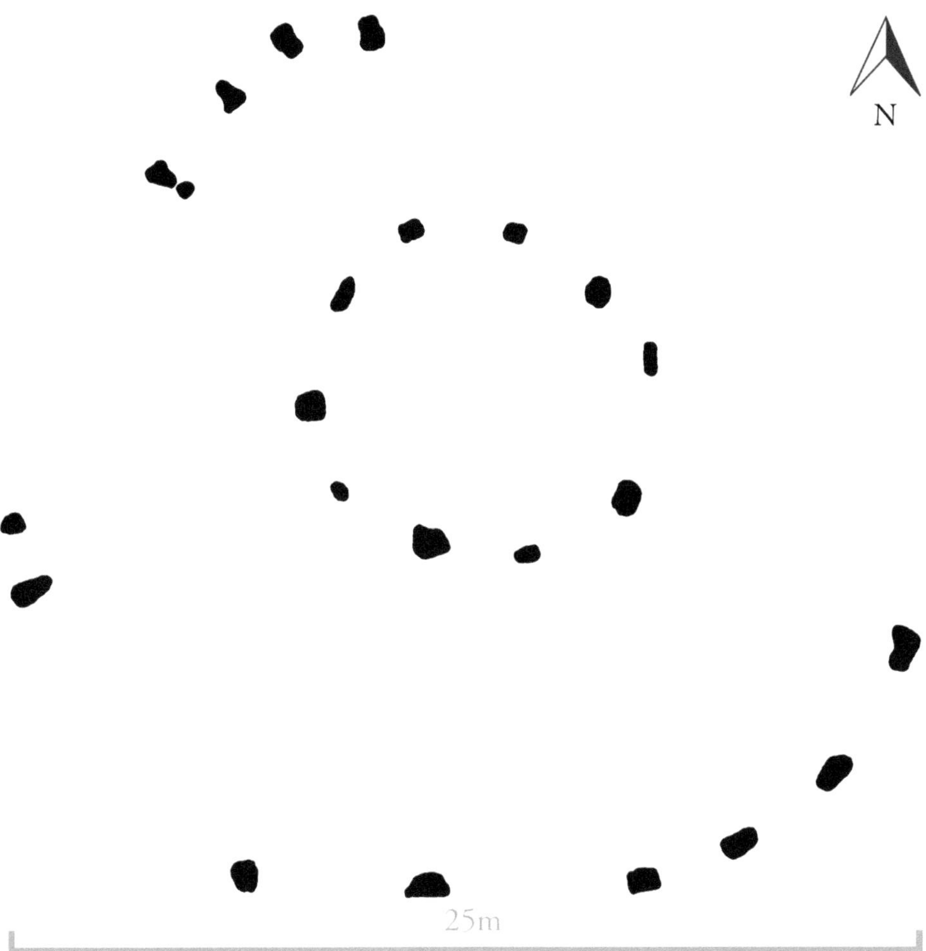

Buried between the inner and outer circles, a ring of cobblestones was unearthed, formed in two distinct layers, one above the other. This was likely a ring cairn, a circular embankment of loose stones, typically dating to the Early Bronze Age. Ring cairns are explained in detail in Chapter 3, but simply put, these are thought to have been religious enclosures like stone circles. Unlike stone circles, however, they are almost always associated with cremations and burials.

The multiple layers used to create the ring cairn may suggest that a renovation of sorts occurred at the site, even before the stone circle was added. Beginning its life as a ring cairn, likely used to enclose cremations, Birkrigg evolved to become a more complex enclosure over time. Multi-stage megalithic sites, renovated over several centuries, were common across Bronze Age Britain (Stonehenge being the best-known example, which itself is a concentric stone circle).

Author's Notes: Like all captivating mysteries, Birkrigg remains unsolved. However, since it exists within a Bronze Age cemetery, and several burials were found at its centre, we can deduce that it was used to prepare bodies for the afterlife. Perhaps vital was the discovery of a flat stone around the inner circle, which was found adjacent to the inner circle, under the upper level of cobbling. Large stones like this were feasibly used as excarnation platforms, areas to remove the flesh from a body prior to cremation. This is not an abnormal find at a concentric stone circle. For further context, read the section on Oddendale Stone Circle in Chapter 4, where excarnation platforms are discussed in more depth.

To lend credence to this, a disk-like tool was discovered near the slab. Sharpened around its outer edge and made of sandstone, this disk is thought to have been used as a cutting device. Sandstone is a soft rock, easily honed and fractured. This would suggest that the disk was not used to cut down trees or break bone – instead, as antiquarian Canon Greenwell insisted, this was an instrument created to cut meat or soft material.

GREAT URSWICK BURIAL CHAMBER

This Stonehenge-esque arrangement of stones is located just off a footpath to the west of Great Urswick. Two limestone cubes support a lintel, forming what looks like an entrance way. Despite its name, there is no consensus as to what the Great Urswick Burial Chamber is. It is believed by some to be the remaining facade of a large stone-faced burial monument, not unlike those common in Neolithic Wales. The gap at its centre may have been deliberately aligned with the winter solstice sun, the sun's rays beaming onto the deceased once a year.

Behind the facade is a square enclosure made of several smaller limestone blocks: the eponymous burial chamber. Due to being so dilapidated, there is no way to

– GREAT URSWICK BURIAL CHAMBER –

– COMPARED TO A PERSON OF AVERAGE HEIGHT –

visualise how it would have looked when complete. It possibly once appeared like a smaller version of the better known Bryn Celli Ddu in Wales, with a mound of earth forming its shape.

The structure has the appearance of a dolmen, the ruins of a single-chambered tomb that has had its outer mound removed. Dolmens typically date to the Early Neolithic and are the remains of one of Europe's oldest megalithic traditions: the construction of passage tombs. The Great Urswick Burial Chamber is possibly the only known example of such a monument in Cumbria. That is, of course, if this is considered a genuine prehistoric monument at all. Most academics believe it to be a natural feature.

Simply listed as burial chamber on OS maps, passing visitors might be disappointed to find it in such a ruinous state. It is located next to a limestone outcrop making it hard to distinguish to an untrained eye. This has led numerous archaeologists to doubt its legitimacy, as it blends in rather well with its natural surroundings.

Doubts notwithstanding, there is reliable evidence to suggest that the Great Urswick Burial Chamber is a man-made structure. The limestone blocks are secured in place at their base using loose stones, suggesting that they had been intentionally moved here. A bronze dagger was also discovered in the immediate vicinity, which at least indicates that a prehistoric community was living nearby.

SKELMORE HEADS

Just north-east of the Great Urswick Burial Chamber is the Skelmore Heads Long Barrow. It can be easily accessed via a footpath south from the nearby road.

Long barrows are elongated burial mounds. They are the long Neolithic equivalent of the more prevalent Bronze Age round barrow. As a rule of thumb: if a burial mound is round, it is presumably Bronze Age, if it is long, it *may* be Neolithic. Although there are more than 500 long barrows in Britain, only eleven examples survive in Cumbria, all of which are made of stone. Precisely why these monuments were built from stone in Cumbria is unknown, but earthen examples are far more prevalent in the south of England.

It is located next to the large Skelmore Heads 'Hill Fort', an enclosure thought, by most, to date to the Iron Age (800 BC–AD 100). The date of this enclosure remains controversial, however, and some have speculated, that like the long cairn, Skelmore Heads Hillfort is of Neolithic origin.

Excavations of the barrow in 1933 uncovered just a burial urn and some loose bones, and re-excavations in 1957 revealed the site had been looted some time in its past. The trench dug by the looters can still be seen between two standing stones, which protrude from the top of the mound. These stones are thought to be the remains of a stone row that once ran along its spine. While only two of these stones remain, it is thought that there were originally four. A similar Neolithic burial monument in eastern Cumbria, Raiset Pike, likewise had rows of posts along its length.

As well as the long barrow itself, Skelmore Heads was seemingly once a bustling hub of ancient activity. Excavations at the hill fort unearthed a myriad of artifacts, including several rough Langdale axes and five Bronze Age axe heads. These finds suggest that the area was used to trade axe heads throughout prehistory, possibly later to be shipped overseas.

Skelmore Heads' out-of-place nature, and its proximity to Great Urswick Burial Chamber, suggest that it may be the work of a migratory culture. Both styles of burial monument, more numerous in Wales and Ireland, are rarely seen elsewhere in Cumbria. Their location on the Furness Peninsula is also the closest point in Cumbria to Wales. A cultural influence may have occurred sometime during the Neolithic period, as trade over the sea allowed a subtle transfer of traditions to manifest.

ST BEES

The St Bees coast is the name we will use to define the coastline between the towns of Ravenglass and Maryport. Bronze Age stone circles were once abundant in the region, but as evidenced by the recent destruction of several stone circles, the prehistoric sites here have had a tumultuous relationship with landowners.

The St Bees coast features several sites that demonstrate the idea of stone circle restorations, where the community bands together to re-erect megaliths as their ancestors did before them.

In this respect, the stone circles here show the impact people have had on their heritage, for both the positive and the negative. Of the four stone circles listed in this section, three of them are either semi or fully restored. These have ranged from amateur efforts, to fully funded academic study and restoration. Without this work, it is unlikely that any stone circles on the St Bees coast would have survived the Victorian period. The care taken to preserve these circles, no matter how misguided, has allowed enthusiasts and historians to gain a valuable insight into the area's heritage.

– ST BEES COAST –

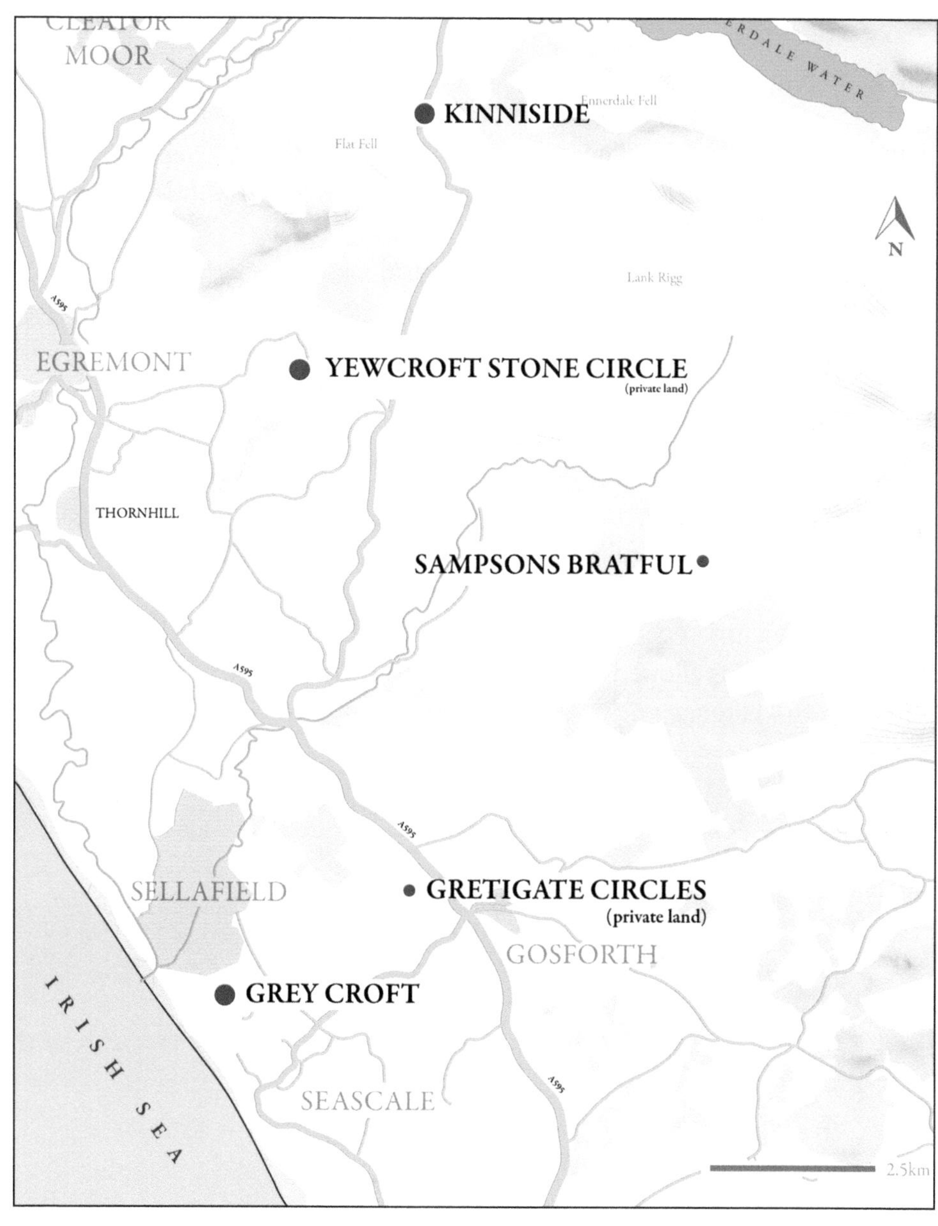

GREY CROFT

Grey Croft is a large burial circle consisting of ten large boulders. Situated in a field adjacent to Sellafield Nuclear Decommissioning Site, it is an incredibly out-of-place collection of stones: an inspiring reminder of how far technology has evolved in the last 4,000 years.

It is safest to walk via the nearby Seascale Golf Club to view Grey Croft, as you can easily spot the circle from the 12th hole without getting too close to Sellafield. Hopping a stile on the fence is allowed for a closer view, though please bear in mind that Sellafield security will remove visitors if warranted.

A good portion of Grey Croft's original charm has likely been lost. Between being buried by a farmer back in the nineteenth century and a nuclear power plant being built on its doorstep in the 1950s, Grey Croft is a site for only the hardened stone circle enthusiasts. It certainly isn't situated in the most serene location, and the knowledge that you are being watched from the guard towers along the perimeter wall of Sellafield can make this a rather intimidating experience.

– GREY CROFT STONE CIRCLE AND SELLAFIELD –

– GREY CROFT
DIAGRAMMED FROM ABOVE –

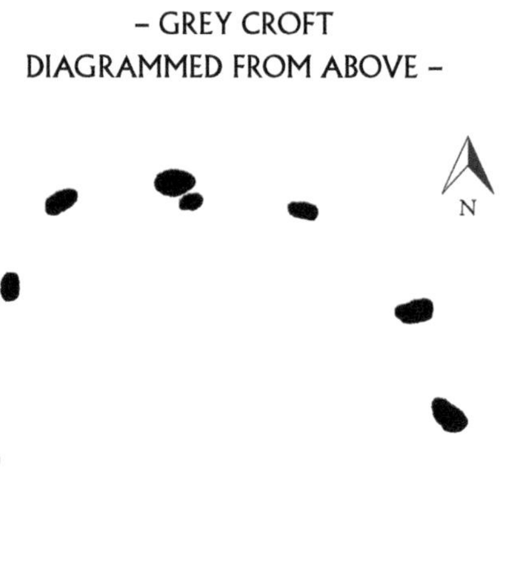

An excavation in 1949 unearthed a round cairn at Grey Croft's centre, containing several artifacts. Among the finds were: a jet ring (possibly an import from the continent), a Langdale axe head, and small tools dating to the Neolithic period. This does not necessarily indicate that Grey Croft was a Neolithic circle, but it does prove that people had settled at this specific location for centuries throughout prehistory.

Grey Croft seemingly had a varied history of uses. On the eastern edge of the circle, a Langdale axe head was discovered next to a stone, which suggests people settled here during the Neolithic period. Later, during the Early Bronze Age, the round cairn was added – possibly to bring the circle up to style with others on the coast (such as Birkrigg).

Excavated bone fragments from within the cairn revealed evidence of intense burning. In places, a layer of sand found throughout the inner area of the circle was fused together like glass, strongly suggesting that Grey Croft was another stone circle used during cremations. Perhaps the question that should be asked is:

Were those cremations occurring specifically for the one person buried in the centre of Grey Croft? Or was this site continuously used for cremation throughout the Bronze Age?

Nobody knows for certain, but the evidence suggests that multiple people were interred into these circles over the course of several hundred years.

In 1820, the tenant farmer, James Fox, buried all but one of the stones while the landowner was away on business, presumably to make way for his plough. A heavily damaged stone, found at the western edge of the circle, is also believed to have been struck by Mr. Fox with a sledgehammer. The stones remained buried until the year 1949, when Fletcher restored the circle with the help of local schoolchildren.

This begs a question: how do you want to be remembered? Mr Fox certainly did not want this one humiliating anecdote to be his lasting legacy, which makes his actions all the more tragic. Perhaps Grey Croft should serve as a cautionary tale of why, precisely, it should be in everyone's best interest to preserve and care for our historic monuments. Lest we be remembered like the fantastic Mr Fox.

KINNISIDE

Kinniside is a small stone circle situated under Blakely Raise Fell. It is one of two restored stone circles east of Cleator Moor, the other being Yewcroft.

Accessing Kinniside stone circle is easy since it is located mere metres from the road. You can park opposite the circle and look on from the comfort of your driver's seat if you are so inclined. It is just one of several Bronze Age monuments that can be found on this open moor overlooking Egremont. Several settlements and burial cairns were built further up the hill next to the River Calder, a source of fresh water that was likely the reason people first settled here.

Kinniside is a reconstructed stone circle, as evidenced by its loving nickname 'Fakeley Raise Stone Circle'. Sometime during the eighteenth century the circle was deconstructed by a local farmer, who used the pillaged stones as gateposts. It was recreated in 1925 by Dr Quine, who re-erected the stones and set them

- KINNISIDE STONE CIRCLE DIAGRAMMED FROM ABOVE -

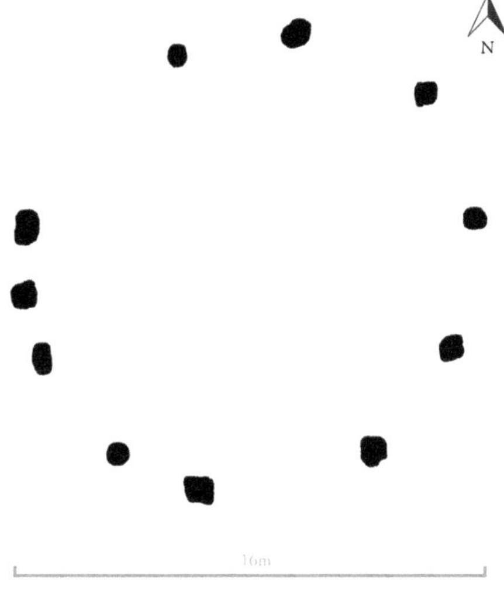

in concrete. Unfortunately, his reconstruction was not supervised by any archaeologists, and there is little evidence to indicate that all the stones belong to the original circle. Hunting for alignments here is not advisable for this reason.

Botched restoration aside, Kinniside is presumably not too unrecognisable from how it once stood, and its size and position in the landscape is not disputed. It bears a striking resemblance to the White Moss stone circles found on Burnmoor and Lacra B on Lacra Bank. Not only did it originally contain the same number of stones – but it also had the same width of 16 m. This style of stone circle is deeply connected to Early Bronze Age burial rituals, as evidence found at Burnmoor and Grey Croft shows that there were cremations taking place within the centre of these circles over multiple generations.

Author's Notes: Because there is little record of Kinniside prior to its reconstruction, it is unknown if a central burial cairn like those at Burnmoor sat at its centre. If we were to speculate, we could imagine this was a burial monument like White Moss, Low Longrigg and Lacra B, all coastal circles built on upland moors.

STUDFOLD

A large but ruinous stone circle, Studfold can be found near a small patch of woodland just south-east of the village of Gilgarran. It is located just below the brow of a small hill, which makes it impossible to observe without venturing into the field. It is on private land and is likely not visited often, so make sure to seek the landowner's permission if you want to visit.

The circle has been cut in two by a dry-stone wall, and most of it now sits within a bog, making it invisible to all but the local frogs. Luckily, the stones on the east side of the wall are still standing and appear to remain as they originally did in the Early Bronze Age. The wall is clearly the worse for wear, and stretches of its length have toppled over, seemingly due to the inclusion of several of the circle's stones in its construction.

Like other stone circles on the St Bees coast, Studfold contains an inner burial cairn. The presence of this cairn indicates that Studfold was connected to Early

– THE LARGEST STONE AT STUDFOLD, NOW COVERED BY A WALL –

– STUDFOLD STONE CIRCLE DIAGRAMMED FROM ABOVE –

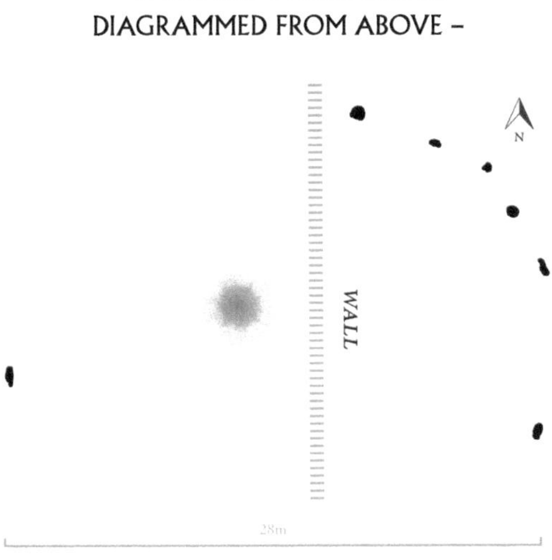

Bronze Age burials, although it appears unlike Grey Croft or Kinniside. Studfold was, perhaps instead, a site comparable to Brat's Hill on Burnmoor. Like Brat's Hill, Studfold is a wide stone circle containing inner burial cairns made up of low-lying stones. With such a remarkably similar appearance, it could be argued that Studfold was possibly once part of a complex of monuments like those at Burnmoor. Considering the destruction of the circle at the hands of previous landowners, other monuments in the area would likely have been removed also, leaving only Studfold and its singular cairn.

Antiquarian J.R. Mason surveyed and probed the circle in 1925, finding a central cairn and multiple buried stones. Several Gilgarran locals showed him stone tools that they had unearthed while digging, and possibly even a polished stone axe. Whether or not these were related to the circle is not known, but their presence certainly indicates that people occupied the area since the Neolithic.

YEWCROFT

Yewcroft is the most recently restored stone circle listed in this book. It can be found in a private field south-east of the small village of Wilton. Like Kinniside, it is a nearly completely restored stone circle, although in this case there appears to have been far more care put into its reconstruction.

Wilton was awarded funds in 2000 to create a report on their village history. During research, a map dating to 1777 was uncovered among a landowner's deeds. In a field known as Yewcroft Meadow, a feature had been clearly labelled as a Druidd Temple. Until this discovery, no such circle had been known to exist, leading to a quick survey and excavation at the site in 2012. Eleven conspicuous pink granite stones were found in a nearby hedge, and over the course of four days, they were rearranged into the circle we see today.

The reconstruction was supervised by Professor Terence Meaden, a megalithic scholar, and a well-known voice in the study of stone circles. In his diary he

– YEWCROFT AS SHOWN ON THE 1777 MAP –

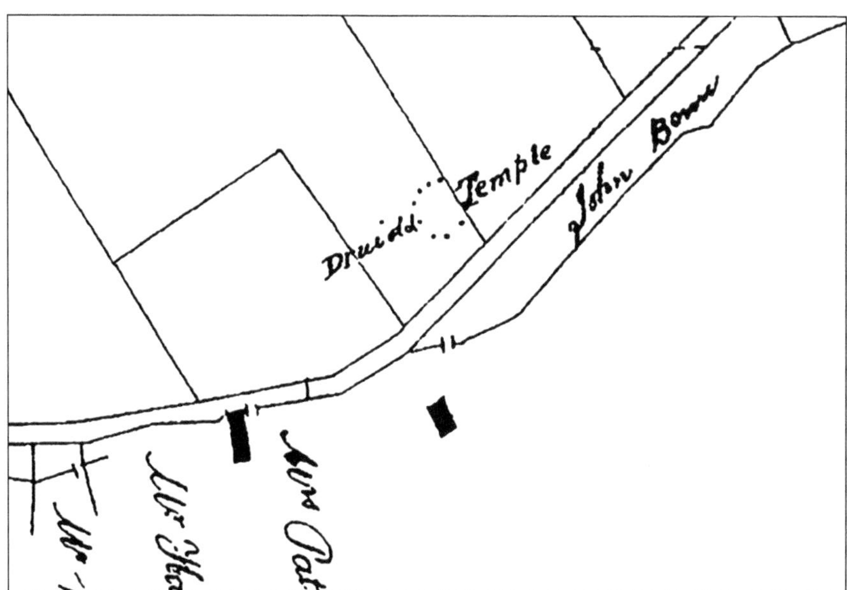

posits that the circle probably dated to 3000 BC to 2000 BC. He also identified a white outlying stone to the north-east of the circle, which he believed was possibly used to align Yewcroft towards the summer solstice sun.

The size of the stones and their oval arrangement are remarkably like Grey Croft, a burial circle. Therefore, one could assume Yewcroft was a burial monument. However, no indication of a burial cairn was unearthed during the 2012 excavation indicating that, although still conceivable, it is doubtful that a burial circle ever stood in Yewcroft Meadow. According to Professor Meaden, Yewcroft was 'no burial monument but a fine traditional stone circle'. Taking Yewcroft's proposed alignments with the solstice sun into account, we may be looking at a site akin to Elva Plain.

Author's Notes: Regardless of the original builders' intentions, there is no doubt that Yewcroft is a wonderful sight to behold. This area has been greatly improved by the restoration, and the work involved has created a landmark that will undoubtedly stand the test of time. As online personality Tom Scott explained when discussing Avebury's restoration: '*Nobody complains when the Sistine Chapel is restored every now-and-then, and I don't think that we should complain that these stones have been restored either.*'

THE MILLOM PENINSULA

The Millom Peninsula boasts numerous intriguing sites, all of which are located under the iconic Black Combe Fell. This rolling hill dominates its surrounding landscape, overlooking the entirety of the Cumbrian coast from north to south.

Modern research has yet to be fully undertaken on the Millom Peninsula, and most sites have yet to be excavated. The period in which the megaliths were erected, and in what order, remains a mystery. Even the best-understood monuments have conflicting historical reports, and the limited excavations here have failed to find even a shred of evidence pertaining to their origin. For these reasons, the area has become something of an archaeological black hole.

Despite the unanswered questions, researchers know that a large prehistoric community settled here, who created colossal sites like Swinside Stone Circle with an incredible level of skill. Unfortunately, the ravages of time have reduced the region's prehistoric legacy down to wisps of mystery. All that remains are the megaliths, and the questions they beg to have answered.

- THE MILLOM PENINSULA -

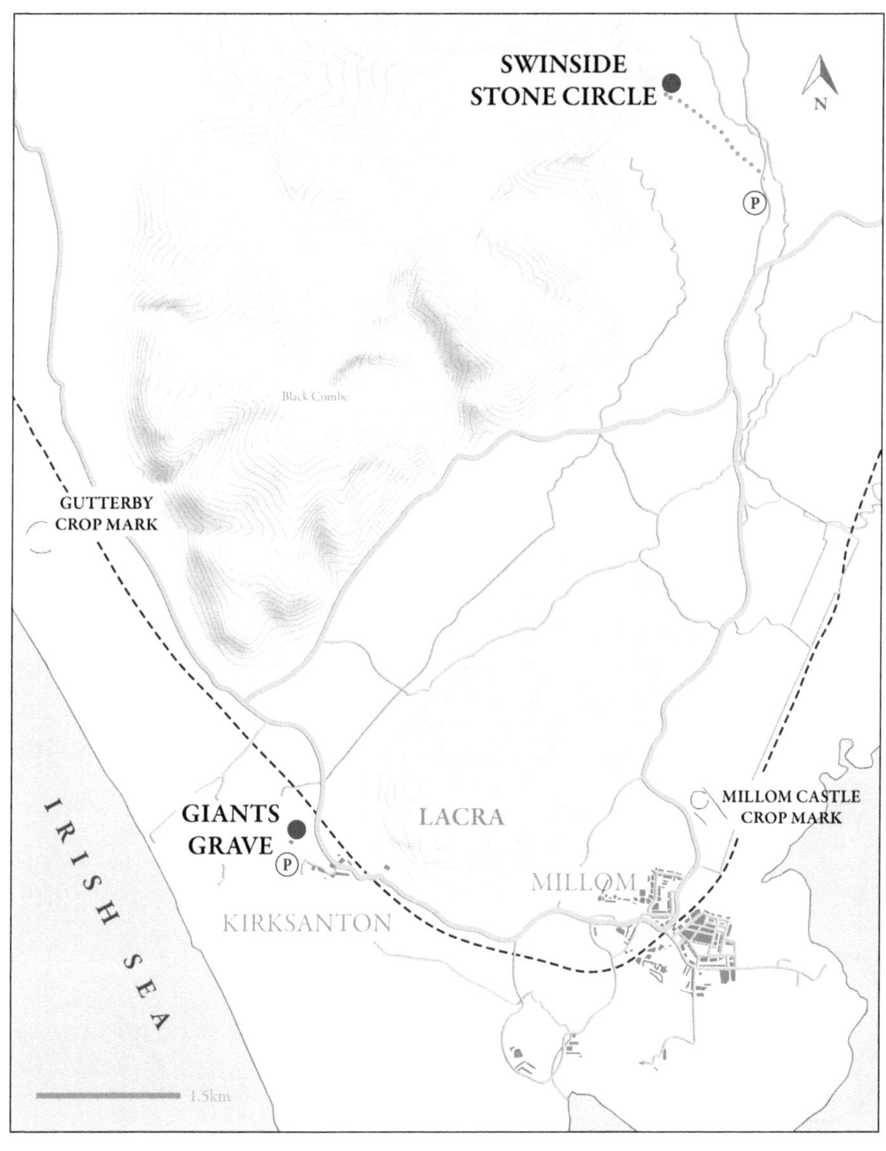

THE MILLOM LINES

Strange reports began to emerge from the skies over Millom during the 1980s. Pilots told tales of large speckled circles that appeared to grow into the crops below. An adventurous mind may have instantly recalled images of UFO films, such as *Signs* or *Close Encounters of the Third Kind*, but with the advent of easy to access aerial photography a clearer picture began to emerge.

The Millom Lines are crop marks, a phenomenon which occurs when crops dry out in shallower soils, in this case revealing where trenches were dug deep into the bedrock. Six of these circular crop marks are found along the coast, forming a chain that stretches all the way from Millom Castle up to Bootle. The most elaborate collection appears to be at the Giant's Grave, where three circles appear in a row, one possibly containing the remnants of a cursus monument, an extremely ancient earthwork (which are covered in further detail in Chapter 5).

The crop mark circles are each 64m in diameter, containing a ring of circular marks around their inner perimeter. These inner marks are post holes, niches in the bedrock where posts were once placed. Considering that there are no stones standing on the crop marks today, we can assume that these circles were created

– THREE OF THE MILLOM LINE CROP MARKS –

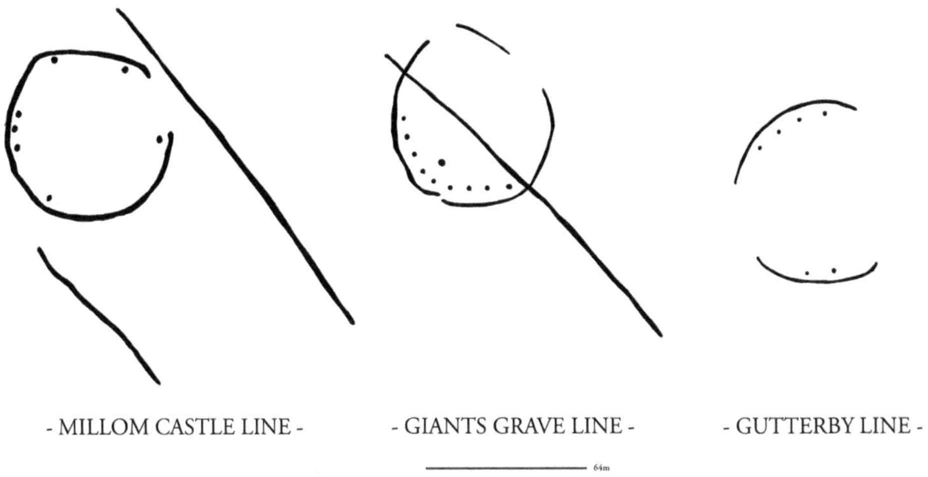

- MILLOM CASTLE LINE - - GIANTS GRAVE LINE - - GUTTERBY LINE -

64m

using wood. These monuments, typically known as timber circles, were generally created during the Neolithic, and often pre-date megalithic monuments. Sadly, any timber posts would have quickly rotted away, leaving only traces of the post holes in which they stood.

Clearly these circles were created by a people of great antiquity, but two key questions remain: *When were they created, and why?* Monumental earthwork enclosures like the Millom Lines were created during the Neolithic period, such as at Avebury in Wiltshire and the Ring of Brodgar on Orkney. In this case, however, the lines are rough and the circles made from timber, suggesting that these may be early prototype henge monuments (again, these are further detailed in Chapter 5).

The Millom Lines are possibly the remnants of large Neolithic religious enclosures. During the winter solstice, the ghostly shapes we perceive in the soil today may have been alive with celebration. Communities possibly gathered at these circles every year, witnessing the solstice sunrise and sunset on the horizon. Feasts may have been thrown, maybe honouring those who had died during the past year. This is, of course, all conjecture. But with the size and scope of these henges, it is evident that massive group ceremonies were taking place, and the area surrounding Millom was once bustling with Neolithic activity.

THE GIANT'S GRAVE

Next to the village of Kirksanton, under the gaze of walkers climbing Black Combe, stand two crude megaliths known as the Giant's Grave.

The tallest stone measures 3m in height, while the other stands at around 2.5 m, displaying several cup marks on its side. Despite the name, the Giant's Grave is not a grave, nor was it constructed by giants. Its name is thought to originate from the incorrect belief that a burial mound once existed between the stones. No evidence for this can be found today, and the grave was likely either fanciful conjecture or misidentified furrows from nearby ploughing.

The stones are often described as 'aligning to the summer solstice sunrise', since they point towards the south-west. However, as the recent discovery of the Millom Lines has shown, the Giant's Grave may be only one part of a far larger complex of sites.

During droughts in 2018, the crops in the area dried out revealing a complex of lost Neolithic enclosures in the two adjacent fields. These massive crop marks stand equidistant from the Giant's Grave, possibly indicating that the stones were an element of the Millom Lines. During the winter solstice sunrise, the sun would have streamed between these stones, directing two shadows towards a massive

– THE GIANT'S GRAVE AND BLACK COMBE –

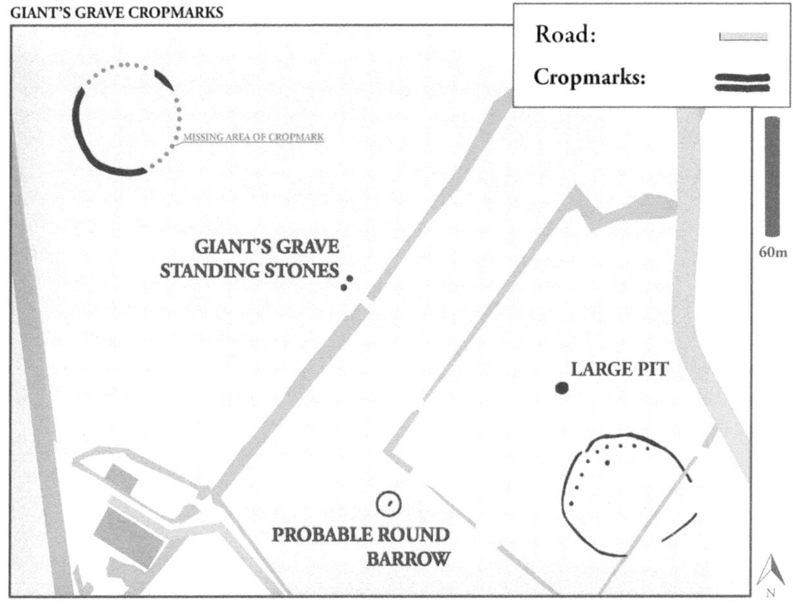

trenched enclosure to the north-west. Conversely, on the summer solstice sunset the shadows would stream towards the enclosure to the south-east.

Directly south-east of the stones is another colossal cropmark, a large dark circular impression. Since dark crop marks indicate where bedrock was removed in the past, this was clearly a large pit of some kind. Whether this was a burial monument, a quarry or an enclosure of some variety is not known, although again, the Giant's Grave appears to align towards its centre.

SWINSIDE

Considered to be one of Europe's best-preserved stone circles, Swinside is a site deserving of intense study. It can be found next to the aptly named Grey Stones Fell, north of Broadgate. Despite being renowned in academic circles, Swinside is rarely visited by the public, presumably because of its remoteness.

Swinside is a stone circle in its archetypal form, a large stone enclosure with no frills. No cairns, earthworks, rock carvings or stone rows can be found within the circle. The views are lacklustre, but the circle alone makes it a contender for the finest prehistoric monument in Cumbria. Fifty-five slate boulders make up its circumference, the largest of which stands 10ft tall. The whole site smacks of authenticity, with only a few stones having fully toppled.

Stone circles of this size are rarely found in such isolation. Instead, they are commonly part of a network of settlements, enclosures and burials. Perhaps important, is a cairn-field 1.6km north of Swinside, known as Lath Rigg. This moor contains over 100 clearance cairns, as well as several hut circles. The cairns on Lath Rigg were not built to specification, or with the intent of a burial – instead they are the product of agricultural landscaping (like those found on Burnmoor). Therefore, we can assume a community of prehistoric farmers,

- SWINSIDE DIAGRAMMED FROM ABOVE -

capable of hauling large boulders, were settling nearby.

Few stone circles match Swinside's size or level of preservation, yet with such a promising site available to study, it is astonishing that there is so little known about its origins. Despite Swinside's links to the Neolithic, the lack of a thorough excavation leaves a lot to be decoded – and the mystery of when it was built, and why, remains.

The first excavation at Swinside was carried out in 1901 by antiquarian C. Dymon, but since then no further digs have taken place. All that was found were modern coins and some evidence of burning, not providing enough information to suggest a purpose for the circle. However, the excavation trench only covered one tenth of the inner area of the circle. The excavation found no trace of human bones or cremated remains, suggesting that this was not a funerary site.

- THE LARGEST MEGALITH AT SWINSIDE -

The lack of post holes or packing stones left by missing megaliths implies that Swinside remains as it did in prehistory.

A specific style of entrance using four large stones opens the circle to the south-east, marking the winter solstice sunrise. Curiously, this style of entrance is only seen elsewhere at Long Meg and Her Daughters, north of Penrith, which could be an indicator of Swinside's age. Long Meg is thought to date to the Neolithic or Early Bronze Age, a period that saw the construction of many large stone circle enclosures. These were made up of massive stones and had an extensive traversable area at their centre. It is assumed that people would gather inside these enclosures for solstice celebrations.

Picture if you will, a cold dark December morning. A Stone Age community has gathered into the centre of Swinside, and sunlight has just begun to fade into the sky. For some time, there is silence. They gaze onto the horizon to the south-east, which is framed perfectly between the stones of the circle's entrance. Slowly, but predictably, the sun – the source of all life on earth – shines directly onto the suspenseful crowd.

It is not known what would happen next, or how the reaction to the sunrise would differ if it were cloudy. But what is clear is this: Swinside allowed Neolithic people to anticipate the sun's path through the sky, signalling a new solar year, and the beginning of the cold winter to come.

Author's Notes: Swinside is a fantastic example of a solar-aligned stone circle, which was likely designed for the purpose of tracking the sun in a way comparable to Stonehenge. For the greatest effect, I recommend that you visit on a winter solstice morning to witness the sun rising through the circle's entrance.

LACRA BANK

Lacra Bank is a Bronze Age funerary complex, as evidenced by the many small burial cairns that dot the hillside. However, Lacra is best known for its stone circles, which can be found scattered around an abandoned farmhouse just below the apex of the hill. Incredible views can be appreciated from these circles, over the sea as far as Ireland, making Lacra Bank a magnificent spot to visit regardless of its archaeological importance.

Despite the ruinous state the circles have been left in, they are still fantastic examples of what can be found in an Early Bronze Age funerary complex. As at Burnmoor and St Bees, these stone circles all contain inner burials, and as such, are classed as burial circles. Similar complexes can be seen at Burnmoor and Birkrigg: plateaued hilltops on which bodies were cremated and buried. Unlike large religious enclosures, such as Castlerigg or Swinside, the stone circles on Lacra Bank were created for the purpose of carrying out funerals.

As well as the burial circles, Lacra Bank is also home to a distinctive stone avenue – an exceptionally rare form of monument in Britain. Only four stone avenues remain standing in Cumbria, making Lacra Bank a fascinating area in the study of Early Bronze Age ritual sites. The avenue, as well as the circles here, seem to have been aligned towards the solstice sun, as is often the case at Early Bronze Age sites (Swinside for example). Complexes like these were possibly used to celebrate the dawn of the summer or winter solstice, and honour those the community lost along the way; multipurpose religious centres for a reasonably sized community.

– LACRA BANK –

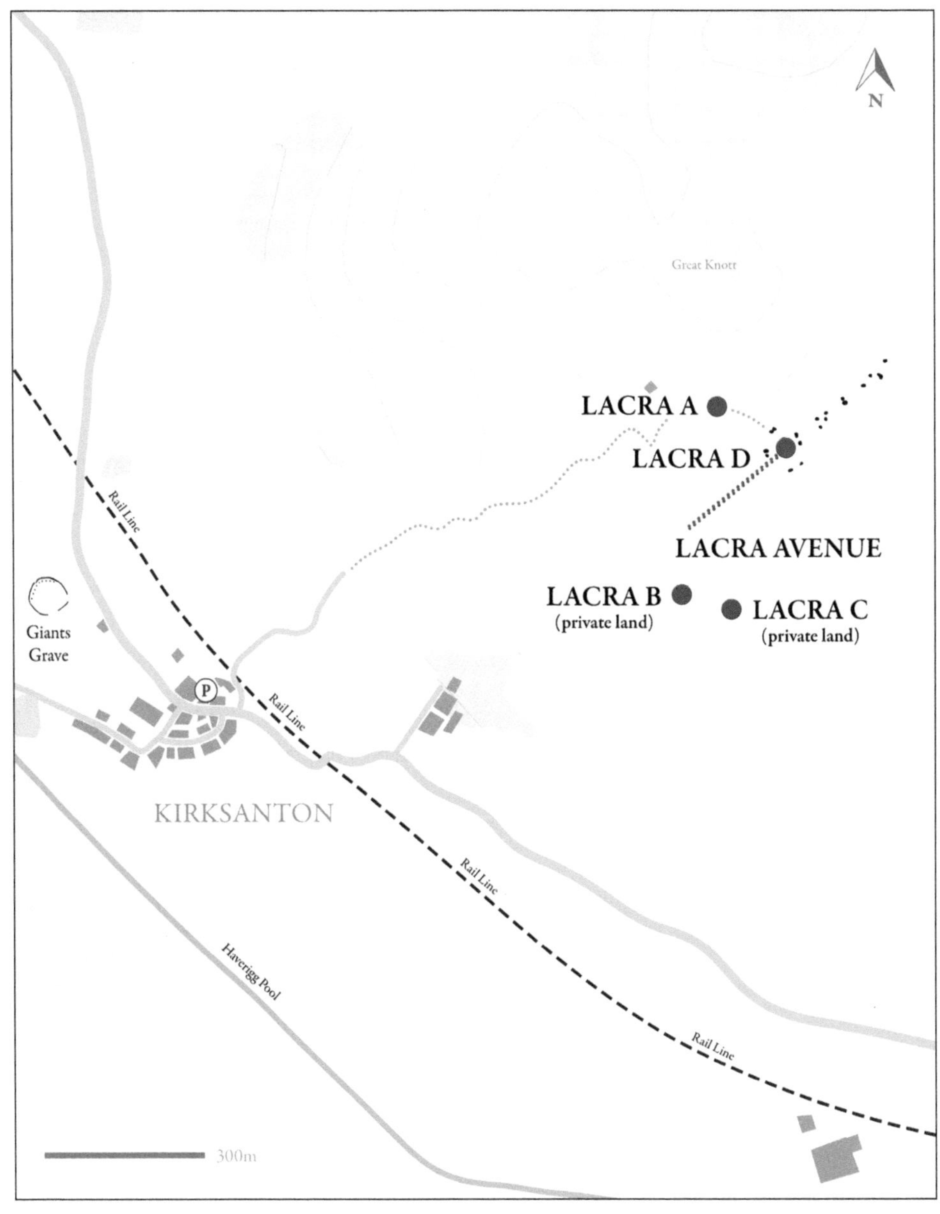

N
Great Knott
LACRA A
LACRA D
LACRA AVENUE
LACRA B
(private land)
LACRA C
(private land)
Rail Line
Rail Line
Rail Line
Rail Line
Giants
Grave
P
KIRKSANTON
Haverigg Pool
300m

LACRA AVENUE

Stone avenues are believed to have been created during the Early Bronze Age, when large monuments are thought to have been created for use in religious ceremonies. Lacra Avenue is possibly one such monument, although its authenticity has been called into question.

Cumbrian avenues, although rare, typically include multiple stone circles along their length. Lacra Avenue is no different, and at its centre stands Lacra D, a messy circle consisting of seven fallen stones. Despite how interesting it may sound on paper, Lacra D is so ruinous that it is almost unrecognisable as a monument. Perhaps its only redeeming feature is the massive capstone that lies at its centre. Capstones are large slab-like boulders that were used as a lid for cist burials, not unlike a modern coffin lid (although much heavier). While often described as such, there is no evidence that Lacra D's inner stone is really a capstone, or just a misplaced boulder; either option is plausible given the circle's dilapidated state.

– LACRA AVENUE'S NORTH END –

– THE NORTHERN PORTION OF LACRA AVENUE –

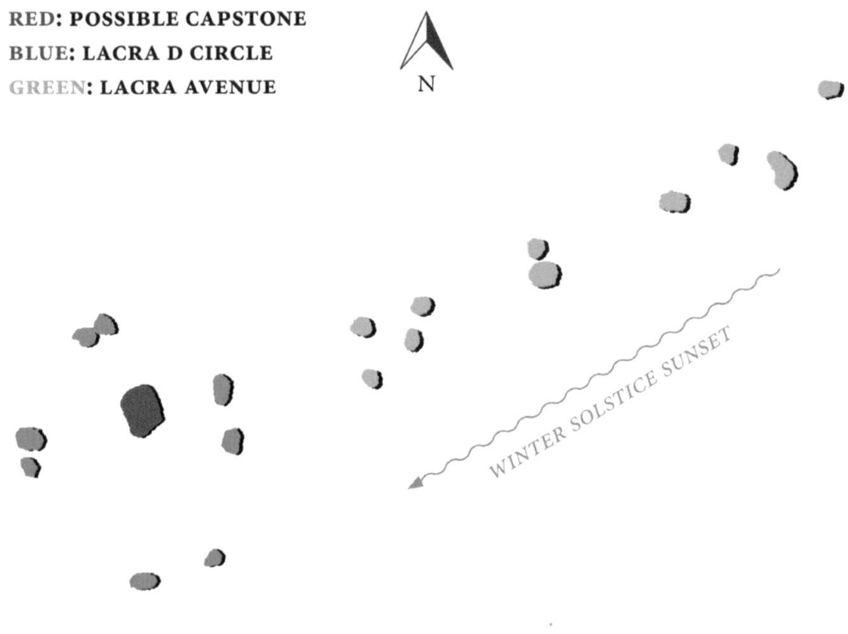

As defined by renowned archaeologist Aubrey Burl, stone avenues come in four distinct forms; only two of which exist in Cumbria:

1. **Type 1 avenues:** short, straight rows of stone.

2. **Type 2 avenues:** long, winding rows of stone.

Lacra Avenue is a Type 1 avenue, with a short span and straight path. This is the most common style of stone avenue in Britain, and one of several on the west coast of England. Interestingly, Lacra Avenue shares several features with the Type 2 Shap Avenue in Eastern Cumbria – the most notable being its alignment, two stone rows running parallel towards the solstice sun.

Avenues may have been the Early Bronze Age counterparts of Neolithic cursus monuments, long earthen enclosures that were used for unknown purposes. To what extent these megalithic monuments drew influence is not known. Their size and shape suggest that processions took place within their length, not unlike the aisle of a church or a parade ground.

Talk that Lacra Avenue was, perhaps, not as man-made as it first appeared, emerged in 1999. English Heritage field investigators concluded that the avenue was nothing more than a natural collection of boulders. Features not typically seen at other stone avenues are found in abundance at Lacra Avenue. For instance, the avenue sits lengthways across an incline, causing it to lean. And the way the stones are scattered would have made it an impractical enclosure for ceremonies. The diagram provided in this book can also appear rather misleading. Numerous large stones litter Lacra Bank, and an adventurous mind could easily jump to conclusions. However, some evidence to support Lacra Avenue's human origins has been found during excavations.

In 1947 a large collared urn was discovered beside one of the stones in Lacra D, decorated with a motif typical of the Middle-to-Late Bronze Age (est. 1000 BC). As mentioned earlier, excavations across Britain have revealed that urns were almost always buried with their opening facing downwards, as was the case at Lacra Avenue. Often, the top face of the urn is ornately decorated with circular motifs, as if to present a message upwards, towards the sky.

The burial of this urn was probably not contemporary with the construction of the avenue, but it was possibly buried here long after the site had been established. Urn burials like this are commonly unearthed at Neolithic and Early Bronze Age sites. People of the Mid to Late Bronze Age were often buried near earlier monuments which continued to hold ritual importance.

Of course, this does not definitively prove that Lacra Avenue was created by human hands, it only implies that Middle Bronze Age people believed the stones to be important when this urn was buried. It has been observed several times, at sites such as Copt Howe, that prehistoric Britons would utilise natural features in the landscape if they resembled monuments. In this case, a naturally formed row of stones may have been repurposed as a stone avenue, with Lacra D being the only truly man-built monument along its course.

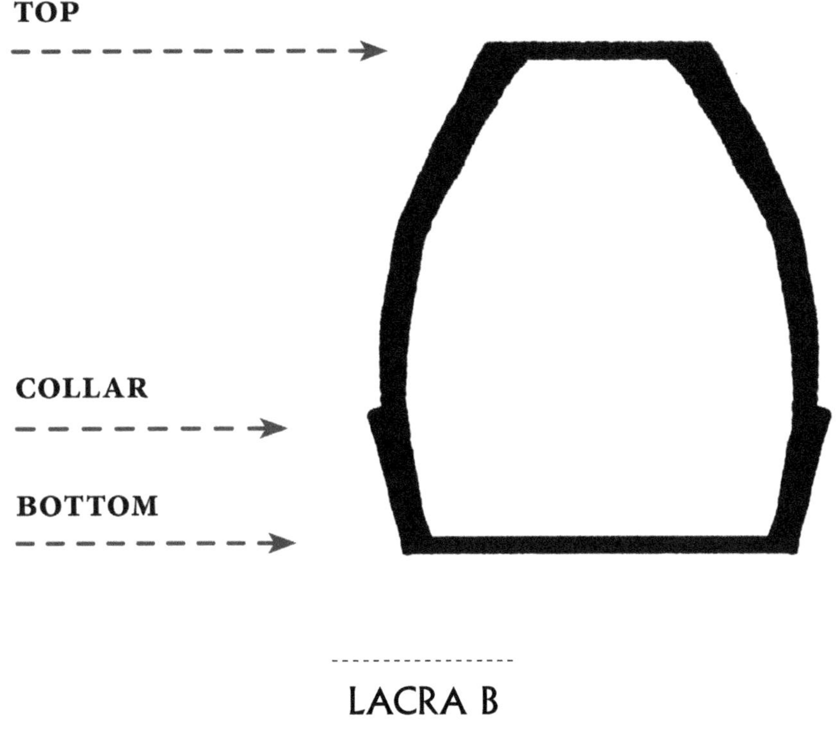

LACRA B

Lacra B is an Early Bronze Age burial circle situated on an open plateau extending views over the Duddon Estuary as far as Walney Island. It sits in a small clearing between four craggy outcrops to the south of Lacra Farmhouse.

Despite having been *literally* blasted in two, Lacra B is the most easily recognisable monument on Lacra Bank and remains quite well preserved. During the Victorian period, the practice of destroying any objects that prevented ploughing was rather common, which was likely the case here in the nineteenth century, when five of the stones were blasted with dynamite. As it stands today, Lacra B consists of only six stones, with excavations finding five additional post holes.

The inner area has an uneven cobbled appearance due to the presence of a small round cairn at the centre of the circle. Stone circles similar to Lacra B, such as those at Burnmoor and St Bees, also surround central burial cairns. While it seems

– LACRA B STONE CIRCLE –

obvious to assume that the stone circle and cairn were built at the same time, some argue that the cairn was, in-fact, added during a later period.

Like those found within Castlerigg, the cairn at Lacra B may have been built for Bronze Age people in an attempt to aggrandise their small burial. A modern equivalent would be having your gravestone placed next to Buckingham Palace; most people would assume you were important based on the location of your grave alone.

– LACRA B FROM ABOVE –

(the blue X's representing the position of the missing stones)

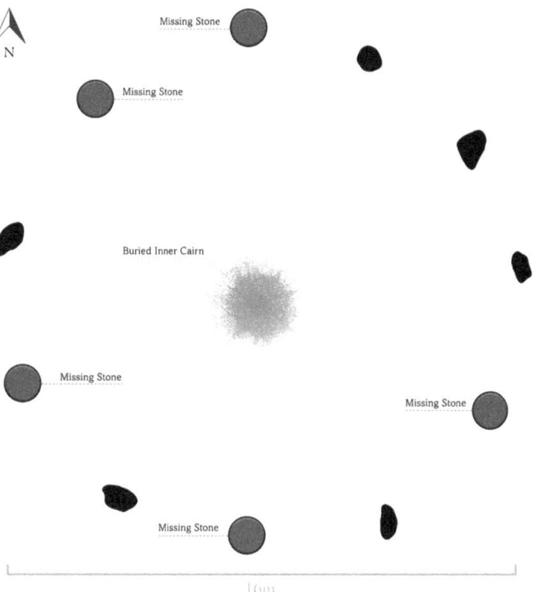

Of course, this was not necessarily the case, and based on circumstantial evidence alone, we can guess the stone circle was created to encircle the burial of an eminent member of an Early Bronze Age community. And in any case, Lacra B had evidently served as a grave immediately prior to being abandoned.

An excavation within Lacra B was carried out in 1948 by Clare Fell, uncovering ashes both inside and nearby the cairn. Fires were clearly raging within this enclosure during prehistory, indicating that cremations took place within the circle. While the presence of such an enclosure on Lacra Bank may seem somewhat mysterious, the reason why people were being cremated here may be obvious. The desire to perform funeral ceremonies in scenic areas is inherent in almost every modern society, and since we are looking at the handiwork of a culture who took their funerals seriously, it is only fitting that this view is so breathtaking.

LACRA A

Lacra A is the closest site to Lacra Farmhouse and is in a similar state of ruin. It sits close to the peak of Great Knott and, like all circles on Lacra Bank, it allows for commanding views over the Irish Sea. Its shape can be hard to discern, as only two stones remain standing of an original seven. As it exists today, eight stones make up the circle. Some are possibly later additions, moved by landowners and placed here to make way for ploughing. A less destructive way to clear a field than dynamite, but infinitely more confusing in this context.

Only five of the stones making up the circle were originally part of the monument. The extra stones may have originated from a once-existent central cairn, which was removed to make way for the plough during the eighteenth or nineteenth century. Therefore, Lacra A is possibly yet another burial circle.

- LACRA A STONE CIRCLE -

LACRA C

The stones of Lacra C were once part of a circle around 20m in diameter. What remains is unimpressive, with only three flat stones lying in a roughly straight line towards the Irish Sea. No human remains or tools were ever found during excavations around the stones, though it is assumed that this is an Early Bronze Age circle. Prior to its near complete destruction, Lacra C was around the same size as Lacra B, and possibly served a similar function as a burial site.

Unfortunately, without concrete answers, Lacra C is simply a row of stones without context. The only indications that the stones were placed by humans are the packing stones. Virtually all prehistoric standing stones were propped up with packing stones, loose stones crammed beside megaliths to keep them from falling. Curiously, because of the lack of packing stones beneath the central stone of Lacra C, researchers know that it sits out of place.

– LACRA C STONE CIRCLE–

OTHER SITES FOUND ON THE COAST

MECKLIN PARK CAIRN FIELD

The Mecklin Park Cairn Field is an expansive collection of cairns found on the fell adjacent to Burnmoor. Mecklin Park is interesting due to the countless archaeological discoveries in the area. While at first thought to be nothing more than an array of clearance cairns, excavations in the 1950s uncovered numerous jewellery, weapons and pottery artifacts (which are now on display at Tullie House Museum in Carlisle).

GRETIGATE STONE CIRCLES

The Gretigate Stone Circles are a collection of ruinous monuments in a patch of woodland south-west of the village of Gosforth. They were likely once burial circles like those at Lacra Bank, small circles with inner burial cairns. Since the circles are almost non-existent and positioned on private land, this is not a recommended visit.

WHITROW BECK

Whitrow Beck Stone Circle is among Cumbria's more remote coastal monuments. It is found directly adjacent to the ruins of a Roman settlement, the walls of which were possibly constructed with plundered stones from this circle.

– A BIRD'S-EYE VIEW OF WHITROW BECK STONE CIRCLE –

The question marks indicate the section of the circle covered by later Roman buildings.

Approximately 22m in diameter, it consists of fifteen stones – only eleven of which are now visible due to a Roman enclosure wall covering its western side. Whitrow Beck is certainly an exciting place to explore for a history enthusiast, and if anything, it is a wonderful demonstration of the different layers of history to be found along Cumbria's coast.

KNAPPERTHAW STONE CIRCLE

Knapperthaw Stone Circle can be found on private land to the south of Knapperthaw village. Time has been cruel to this monument and no stones remain standing, leaving only an earthen ring. No excavations have been carried out here, so little is known about its function. It may have been a ring cairn, which is covered in more depth in Chapter 3.

THE PRIAPUS STONE

This gnarled limestone menhir is built into a wall opposite Great Urswick's old church. The Priapus Stone was used in local fertility rituals up until the

– THE PRIAPUS STONE –

nineteenth century, when it used to stand upright in the adjacent field. Despite the initial belief that the Priapus Stone was nothing more than a rubbing stone for cattle, six cup marks have been discovered on its surface, implying that it was erected during the Neolithic period.

BLAKE FELL ROUND CAIRNS

Two large round cairns can be found perched atop Blake Fell, a sloping hill overlooking Loweswater. These Bronze Age round cairns, which are strikingly similar to Dunmail Raise, have been converted to a shelter for fell walkers. The views from here are some of the finest in the Western Lakes, allowing views deep into the Lake District and far across the Irish sea.

SAMPSON'S BRATFULL

Sampson's Bratfull is a large and peculiar cairn, which makes the arduous trek to find it mostly worth it. It is a starfish cairn, a name derived from the arm-like protuberances that sprout from the edges of the cairn's perimeter. Sampson's Bratful is the largest of several burial cairns built across Stockdale Moor, a massive span of moorland below Caw Fell. These are typical burial monuments of the Bronze Age period, although they appear rather crude when compared to similar prehistoric monuments in the Lake District.

ASH HOUSE STONES

The Ash House Stones lie on a plateau overlooking Duddon Sands, just south-east of Swinside Stone Circle. While not obvious today, these stones are the remains of a once large stone circle. We only have a single source for this, the *Topographical Description of Cumberland* published in 1800, which described a wide circle consisting of twenty-two stones. Unfortunately, only two stones remain, both of which have been intentionally toppled. Given its scale, and the sheer size of the stones, we can assume that this was a Neolithic or Early Bronze Age enclosure circle like Swinside, Castlerigg and Long Meg.

The stone found to the south has several deep, grooved marks on its side, seemingly carved at some time of great antiquity. Many people assume that this was a honing stone, and the area used to polish axe heads prior to trade. Sadly, this is probably far from the truth, as these marks were likely left by someone using an iron bar to topple the stone.

KIRKBY MOOR

While Kirkby Moor is perhaps best known for an enclosure known as The Kirk, located at the south end of the moor, the Kirkby Moor round cairn is far more apparent. Laid bare after an excavation in 1846, multiple chambers have been left open to the elements, likely slowly degrading as time goes on. Luckily for anyone visiting the site, the cairn exhibits a rare example of a visible burial cist, with its capstone strewn to the side. Researchers believe the cairn was created in multiple stages, the result of several round cairns being built one on top of another.

– KIRKBY MOOR ROUND CAIRN –

The Kirk itself is a remarkable monument. Today, it is overgrown, and makes for an underwhelming visit on overcast days. However, during the nineteenth century the Kirk was a prominent and impressive circle. A cobbled ring of stones, with neither an entrance nor inner stones, forms a deep enclosure on the moor. It was reported that a stone circle sprouted from its top, in a fashion similar to Casterton Stone Circle (*detailed in the next chapter*). This is what is known as an "embanked stone circle" - a stone circle sitting atop a ring cairn.

A stone avenue, not unlike the one found at Lacra Bank, is also found at the Kirk, trailing off to the north, towards the round cairn. Combined with the area's stunning views and fields of rich purple heather, Kirkby Moor is a highly recommended visit.

GIANTS' GRAVES

Not to be confused with the far larger Giant's Grave at Kirksanton, Giants' Graves is a disfigured round cairn to the north of Kirkby Moor. While conspicuous due to the megalith erupting from the top of the monument, the cairn's iconic shape is largely due to an 1842 excavation. The monument was rifled during the dig, and within its centre was found charred bones. Like at Kirkby Moor, the bones were buried in a style popular during the Early Bronze Age (semi-cremated and interred without urns).

CHAPTER 3

SOUTH CUMBRIA

South Cumbria is an area that we will classify as south of Kendal and east of Ulverston, an area with an extensive human history. Although far fewer ancient monuments have survived here than in other regions of Cumbria, this is not indicative of a lack human presence. It is probable that South Cumbria was once home to a large population during the Neolithic and Bronze Age.

Any thoroughfare from southern England to the north would have reached its narrowest point in South Cumbria, and its position at the centre of Britain would have made this a significant junction in prehistory. While trade routes between Cumbria and other areas of Britain undoubtedly passed through South Cumbria, there is little evidence to show for it. All that remains today are numerous burial monuments, some of them large and others small and unremarkable.

As mentioned in previous pages, survivor bias has played a significant role in our perception of our history, and southern Cumbria is probably the clearest indication of this theory in play. Many of the historic sites in this area are either isolated or in private parks, which can make visiting the prehistoric monuments here difficult.

LEVENS PARK

Levens Hall Deer Park is located on a limestone escarpment just south of Kendal. Inhabited from the Mesolithic period through to Roman times, it was around 2500 BC when Early Bronze Age people began to build numerous burial structures here.

Sitting at its estuary into Morecambe Bay, at the tail end of the River Kent, Levens Park has always been an incredibly habitable location. Considering the vast number of artifacts discovered on the Furness Peninsula, it is well understood that a somewhat large flow of objects was transferred via this waterway. Settlement at Levens Park likely encouraged trade via the Irish Sea, as the River Kent could have allowed an easy transit of goods into Cumbria.

The prehistoric monuments here are located on both sides of the River Kent but are most densely grouped around what is known as Archers Hill, a steep embankment known for its prehistoric arrowhead discoveries. Several ring cairns were built on Archers Hill, though only one is visible thanks to an excavation in the 1960s. Furthermore, a strange earthwork survives to the north of the river, outside the deer park and adjacent to the road. This enormous stone mound is scantly understood, and its origin has not yet been accurately evaluated.

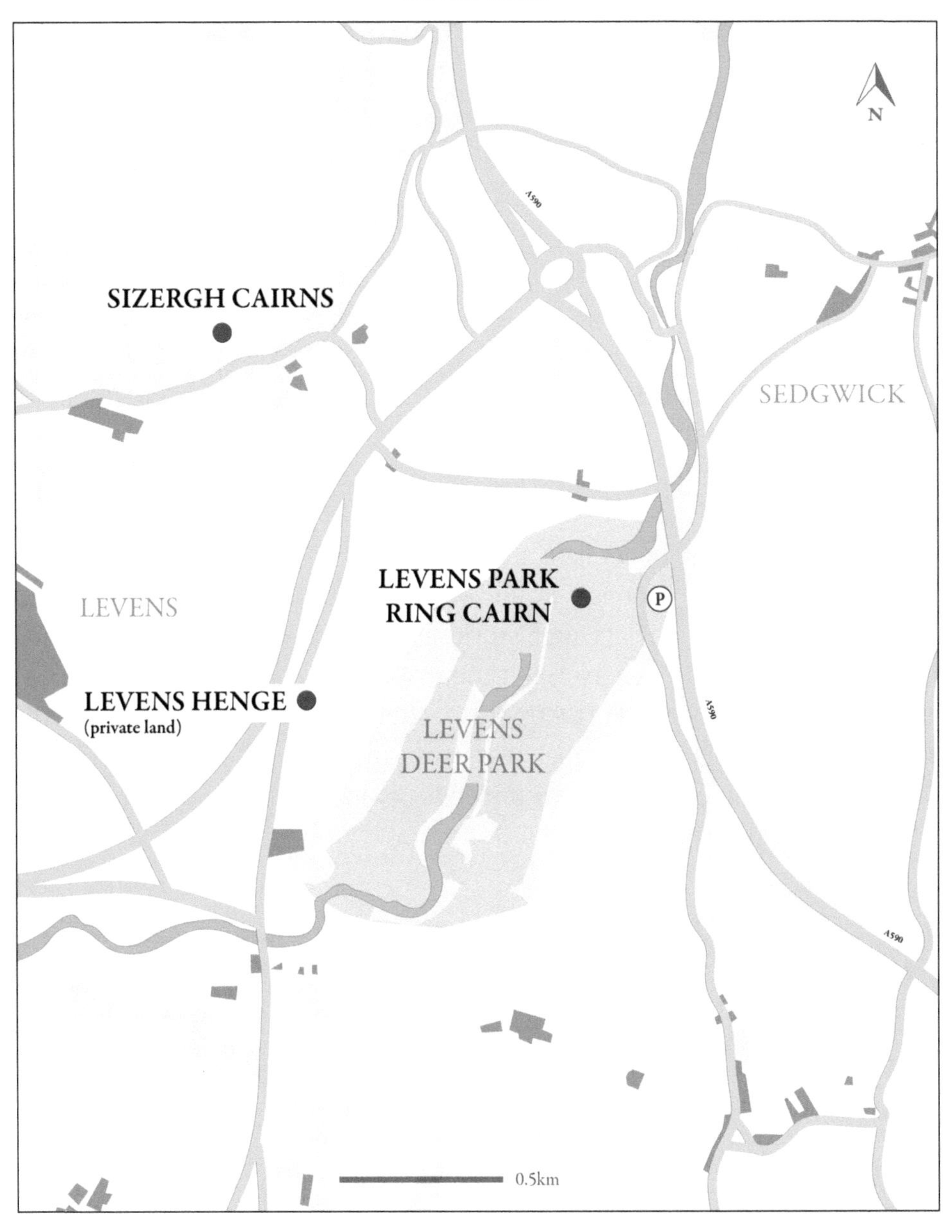
N
A590
SIZERGH CAIRNS
SEDGWICK
LEVENS PARK
RING CAIRN
P
LEVENS
LEVENS HENGE
(private land)
A590
LEVENS
DEER PARK
A590
0.5km

LEVENS PARK RING CAIRN

Levens Park Ring Cairn sits in the north-eastern corner of the deer park, on the edge of Archers Hill. The grass hides a lot of the detail on the monument, but it is easy to make out during the sunrise or sunset.

Ring cairns are circular banks of stone with a flattened area in the middle. Like stone circle enclosures, ring cairns tended to have an open traversable space, which may have been used to hold religious gatherings. They are thought to have been an alternative to stone circles in some regions and were possibly constructed for the same ceremonial purposes. In Cumbria, most ring cairns are either found under concentric stone circles (such as Birkrigg) or completely buried in isolation (such as the Kirk).

While ring cairns may have served as religious enclosures elsewhere across Britain, this cairn is quite distinctly a burial enclosure. The ring cairn encloses four large kerb cairns, not unlike those found at Burnmoor. In fact, the Levens Park Ring Cairn appears to be a ring cairn equivalent of Brat's Hill, a wide enclosure with inner burial cairns. However, Levens Park Ring Cairn seems to have been adapted for different purposes throughout prehistory. Possibly starting as a religious enclosure, it was gradually converted into a burial monument when people chose to be buried within its centre during the Early Bronze Age.

Archaeologist D. Sturdy excavated the cairn in the 1960s, uncovering a wood-lined grave within one of the kerb cairns. Crammed with artifacts, this grave contained three ceramic beakers and two flint knives. The beakers were of a style consistent with the Early Bronze Age, and almost certainly originated from a culture known as the Bell Beaker People. This culture is said to have journeyed across to Britain at the beginning of the Early Bronze Age (around 2500 BC) and are perhaps most famous for their work at Stonehenge.

– LEVENS PARK RING CAIRN FROM ABOVE –

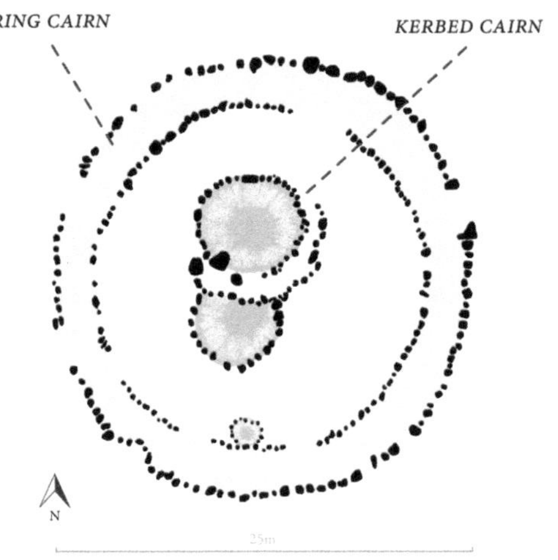

Author's Notes: The best time to visit would be when the sun is low, which shows the cairn at its best. Since the river blocks a northern route to the cairn, you must enter through the deer park's south entrance. The ring cairn is found straight ahead of the gate in an open field. Climbing up the small hill to the south allows a heightened view over the site.

LEVENS HENGE

A yet to be named monument, which we will refer to as Levens Henge, can be found in a private field north of the River Kent. While it is certainly not a henge, it does resemble a miniaturised version of Mayburgh Henge near Penrith. Surprisingly, little is understood about this enormous mound, although it can be compared to a similar monument nearby.

Several researchers have theorised that Levens Henge is simply the remains of a massive round cairn, while others think it is a natural feature. If it is a cairn it should be regarded as among the largest in Cumbria, although most of its volume was quarried during the eighteenth and nineteenth centuries.

It is certainly an eye-catching feature in the landscape, and presumably unnatural. In 1904, archaeologist T. M. Hughes excavated a smaller, but comparable, mound of stone on Sizergh Fell, 1km north of Levens Park. The excavation uncovered several small chambers containing human remains, in a style associated with the Early Bronze Age Beaker People. In total, the bones of nine infants and four adults were extracted from the mound. Levens Henge was probably used in a similar way, to inter the dead.

Archaeologists are particularly talented at identifying burials and associating their customs with a period. Since the burials at Sizergh were placed directly into the cairn without urns, the burials are thought to be Neolithic or Early Bronze Age in origin. However, this does not explain the peculiar shape or large size of these cairns.

– THE MORAINE CAIRN ON SIZERGH FELL –

In the 1960s the area received further study, and the cairns at Sizergh were re-excavated. This time a new conclusion arose. These are **not** man-made cairns – they are instead moraines.

Moraines are natural mounds of loose debris that formed towards the end of the last Ice Age, whereby piles of stone were collected and deposited by glaciers. Cumbria, a landscape that was famously sculpted by glaciers, has its fair share of these rocky mounds. This would surely not have gone unnoticed to a culture with a tradition of cairn burials. So perhaps Levens Henge is just another moraine, converted by prehistoric hands to venerate the dead. Like Copt Howe in Langdale, Early Bronze Age people possibly looked at this natural cairn and saw great potential.

CASTERTON

Casterton is a village to the east of Kirkby Lonsdale, sitting on the border between Cumbria and Yorkshire. Two prehistoric monuments are located on a nearby hill known as Brownthwaite Pike, both of which are distinctly Bronze Age in shape and appearance. Evidence for a small settlement can be seen at the base of Brownthwaite Pike, but whether this was connected to the prehistoric sites is unknown.

The moors surrounding Casterton are among the more isolated prehistoric landscapes in Cumbria. You can spend hours wandering these hills without seeing a soul, making this an excellent spot to visit if you are looking for some peace and quiet. It is thanks to this isolation, that a multitude of archaeological remains have survived on these moors, from Iron Age and Roman settlements, to vast Bronze Age burial grounds.

Brownthwaite Pike sits on Cumbria's border, and technically only one of the monuments exists within Cumbria. Despite this, we will cover both monuments. As with similar upland Bronze Age sites in Cumbria, they were probably intrinsically linked to funeral ceremonies. In this case, there may be a link between these two monuments: two interconnected funerary monuments which served to prepare, cremate and house the bodies of the dead.

Because the area occupies land at the gateway into the Lake District, several trade networks likely passed below Brownthwaite Pike. To support this theory, a jade axe head was discovered outside Casterton in the 1950s. This was an axe head of the Durrington variety, a continental style of axe that may have originated in the Swiss Alps. While Durrington axes are found all over Europe, this is one of the most northerly examples ever discovered.

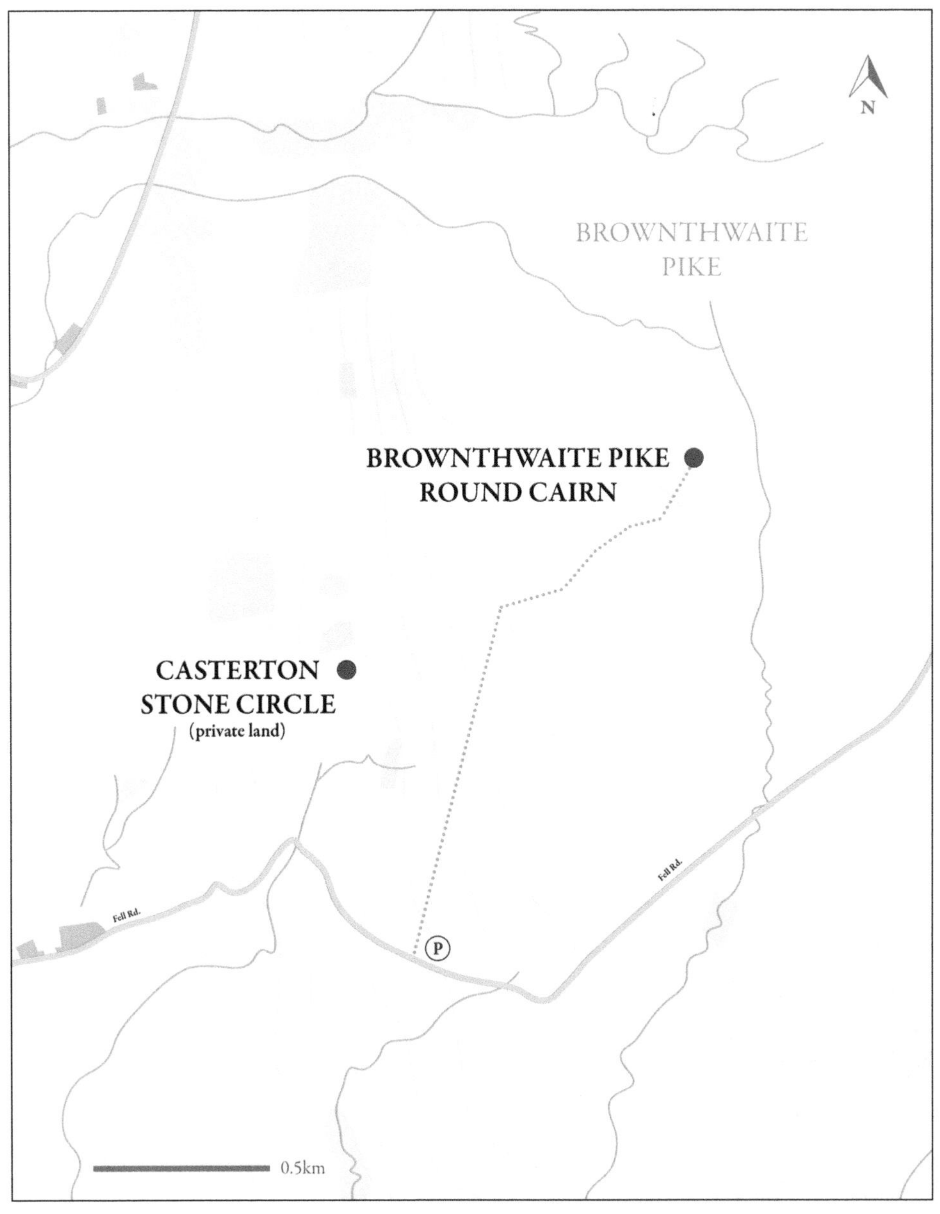
N
BROWNTHWAITE
PIKE
BROWNTHWAITE PIKE
ROUND CAIRN
CASTERTON
STONE CIRCLE
(private land)
Fell Rd.
Fell Rd.
P
0.5km

CASTERTON STONE CIRCLE

Casterton Stone Circle sits at the bottom of a private field to the south of Brownthwaite Pike. Possibly the simplest way to find it is to search for the large earthen embankment on which it sits. It is easily spotted from the footpath leading up the hill.

It has been described as an embanked stone circle. Unlike typical examples of such monuments, Casterton Stone Circle does not sit on a raised ring, but was instead constructed on a large plateaued mound, which gives the site a distinctly disk-like appearance. All the stones are small, so it is unlikely that it was used as an enclosure akin to Swinside or Castlerigg. Instead, it is assumed that this was a circle that served a more specific purpose.

Casterton's low profile implies that it is not a stone circle at all. Instead, it is probably a ring cairn. Ring cairns were created in various shapes and sizes, and a diverse range of designs can be found throughout Britain. They are difficult to discern without an excavation, as their embankments of loose stones are easily covered by earth over time. What we observe today may be simply the most prominent stones of the cairn, sticking up from the dirt (like the points of a buried crown.)

If Casterton is a ring cairn, then it may be connected to Early Bronze Age funerals. As seen at Levens Park and Kirkby Moor, ring cairns were often situated near Bronze Age graves. This is no different at Casterton Stone Circle. Brownthwaite Pike Round Cairn can be easily spotted from the circle, which is believed to be an Early Bronze Age burial cairn. If we were to speculate based solely on circumstantial evidence, we may assume that bodies were either dressed or cremated within Casterton Stone Circle during a funeral, and later buried in monuments like Brownthwaite Pike.

A bronze spearhead and an urn were discovered in the area during the nineteenth century, suggesting that burials were taking place nearby between 2500 BC and 1500 BC. Furthermore, settlement remains dating to the Bronze Age are found to the immediate north of the circle, with Brownthwaite Pike towering over the landscape to the east. It can be assumed that many more monuments once existed on this hillside, but only a few remaining examples have survived.

– CASTERTON STONE CIRCLE FROM ABOVE –

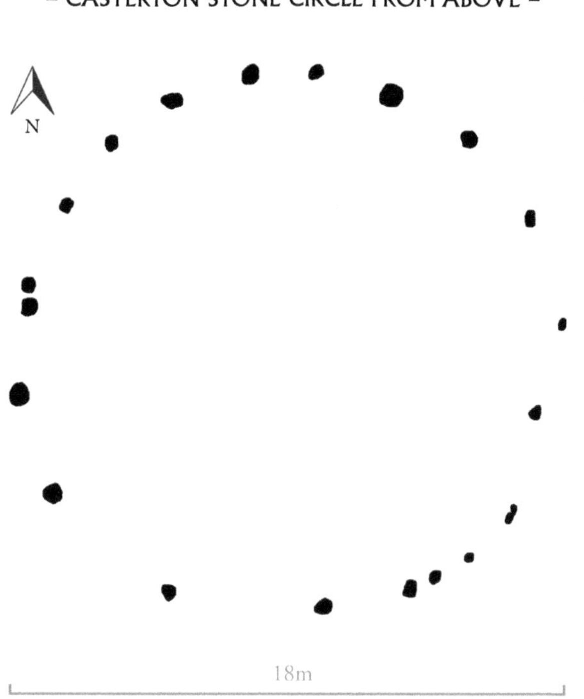

BROWNTHWAITE PIKE ROUND CAIRN

Brownthwaite Pike Round Cairn is a Bronze Age round cairn sitting high above the village of Casterton. A terrific spot to visit if you are looking for a hill walk, the approach from the nearby footpath was one of the steepest encountered in pursuit of photographs for this book (although not quite as steep as Harrison Stickle). A near 45-degree ascent up Brownthwaite Pike allows for clear views all the way to Morecambe Bay to the west and vistas over North Yorkshire to the east: a stunning site to behold.

This is a round cairn like Dunmail Raise, a mound of stones which likely contains the bones and cremated remains of multiple people. No known excavations have been carried out on the cairn, and the lack of a hole indicative of digging indicates that it has not been looted in the past.

It is easy to imagine how the landscape below would have looked back in the Bronze Age. The view from here would have allowed prehistoric people to observe travellers crossing between the north and south of England. Unfortunately, looking down the west coast, south from Brownthwaite Pike, the number of surviving prehistoric monuments begins to decline. This epic cairn may represent the most southern extent of Cumbria's prehistoric monuments.

Whether or not Brownthwaite Pike Round Cairn is related to Casterton Stone Circle immediately down the hill isn't certain, but a sizeable community of people clearly resided in the area during the Bronze Age. Stone circles on the coast were sometimes used to cremate bodies before interment inside round cairns, which again may have been the purpose of Casterton Stone Circle: an area used for funerals before bodies were interred inside round cairns like this.

Standing 9.5m across and approximately 2m tall, Brownthwaite Pike Round Cairn is large enough to see for miles around. Years of agriculture and modern tourism have taken their toll on its appearance. Throughout the twentieth century, over half of the mound was removed to create rock shelters for fell walkers on its western side, practically skinning the cairn to only its rough interior.

– BROWNTHWAITE PIKE ROUND CAIRN –

CHAPTER 4

EASTERN CUMBRIA

Eastern Cumbria's rugged landscapes are among the most isolated in the county, boasting the lowest population density in England and the largest stretches of moorland in Cumbria. While unassuming, the area is home to one of the most impressive collections of prehistoric monuments in the UK.

The monuments of Eastern Cumbria are particularly ancient, dating between the Neolithic and Early Bronze Age. There is debate as to why, exactly, this area was so popular during these periods, but the fertility of the land may be the answer. Rivers, springs and lakes adjacent to moderately flat ground, combined with the proximity to major trade networks, likely led to a boom in the region's population. Sadly, mining has greatly lowered the water table since the nineteenth century, and the destruction of the area's limestone geology has irreversibly altered the landscape.

In modern times, Eastern Cumbria serves as a major hub, joining routes between the Lake District, Yorkshire and Scotland. This would also have been the case during the Neolithic. Land-based trade networks from the west would have passed through Eastern Cumbria on their way to Yorkshire or Scotland. As remains the case today with the M6 motorway, cutting directly through Eastern Cumbria, the route of least resistance will always dominate trade routes. With this logic, we can paint a picture of a prehistoric landscape populated with wealthy farmers, whose land is watered by natural springs, constructing megalithic monuments under the shadow of the Lake District's Fells.

While Eastern Cumbria is well known for the monuments surrounding Shap, numerous Bronze Age burial cairns can be found scattered across the area's countless moors. The majority of these are small, single burials, inferior in scale and complexity to those that came before. If you take the time to explore this region, to imagine when and by who these stones were erected, you can begin to appreciate the mindset of humanity in its most ambitious and creative form.

SHAP

The area surrounding Shap is famous for its medieval ruins and industrial chimneys. To those fascinated by prehistoric archaeology however, this landscape is known for one thing: Shap Avenue, a massive stone avenue that may have been ranked among Britain's most impressive prehistoric monuments. So far, seven burial mounds, two ancient settlements and eleven stone circles have been identified in the area surrounding the village of Shap. Despite the destruction of several monuments, Shap still hosts a fascinating collection of prehistoric sites, the likes of which are rarely found elsewhere in Britain.

Shap Avenue is now mostly lost to the ravages of history, but several associated sites can be found scattered around the village's outskirts. These monuments likely date to the Bronze Age period, sitting on the moorlands where prehistoric settlers would have once farmed the land. To the immediate south of Shap, east of Wet Sleddale, are the remains of a prehistoric settlement. The area's wetlands would undoubtedly make this an ideal area to settle, possibly the reason why the population boomed here during the Early Bronze Age.

You can still find several conspicuous megaliths within many of the village's walls. These are believed to have been taken out of the avenue during the eighteenth century and possibly broken up to be used in construction projects. Most of the remaining sites are found on private land, but the most excellent examples are easily accessible from the village via public footpaths. A walk from the village centre up to White Raise, the site of a large round cairn, is easily achievable. From this hill you can see the majority of Eastern Cumbria and envision just how incredible this region must have been during prehistory.

– SHAP –

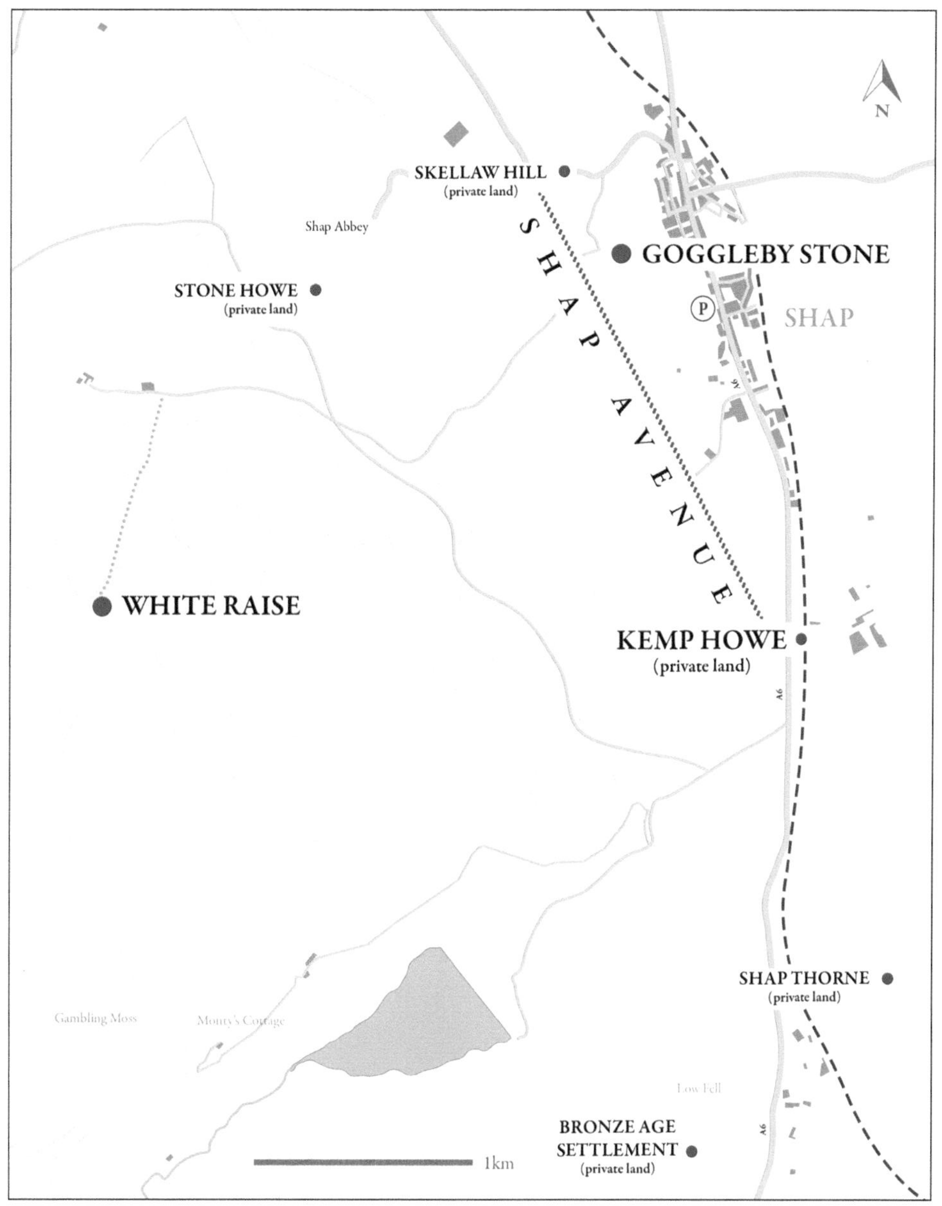

N
SKELLAW HILL
(private land)
Shap Abbey
SHAP AVENUE
GOGGLEBY STONE
STONE HOWE
(private land)
SHAP
WHITE RAISE
KEMP HOWE
(private land)
A6
SHAP THORNE
(private land)
Low Fell
BRONZE AGE
SETTLEMENT
(private land)
1km

SHAP AVENUE

Shap Avenue is perhaps Cumbria's lost wonder of the world. Once a colossal stone avenue, it is speculated to have comprised more than 150 megaliths, arranged into two parallel rows over the length of several miles. Two stone circles are also believed to have been incorporated into its length. Up until its destruction, Shap Avenue was possibly the largest prehistoric monument in Cumbria, a showpiece that attracted so many settlers to the region during prehistory.

It is easy to access the avenue's few remaining stones, and several are found next to public footpaths. Heading south-east from the north-west end of the avenue, you can find the Aspers Field Stone, Goggleby Stone and Giant's Foot megaliths. To the south-east of these stones is Kemp Howe Stone Circle, which marks the end of the avenue. Kemp Howe is the best-preserved portion of the monument, a circle of stones that once formed the bulbous cap to the avenue. In 1844 a rail track embankment was built over it, unfortunately causing the loss of most of the circle. As it survives today, Shap Avenue is only a single row of thirty-one stones surviving over 2.5km.

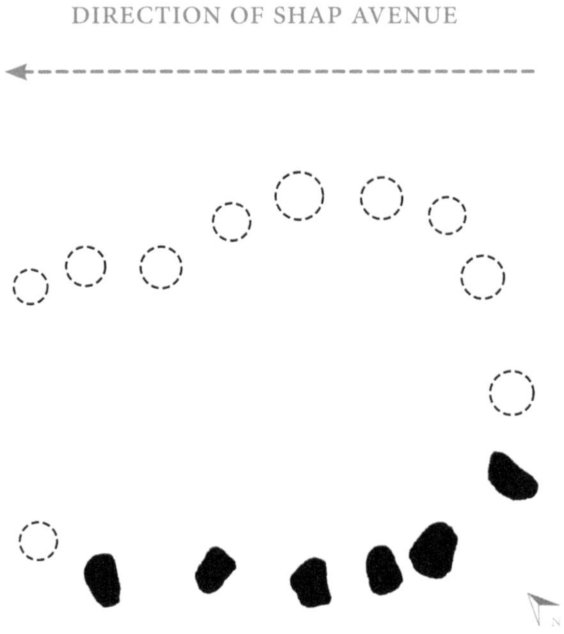

DIRECTION OF SHAP AVENUE

– KEMP HOWE STONE CIRCLE FROM ABOVE –
(the dotted lines represent missing stones)

As with the avenue on Lacra Bank, Shap Avenue likely accommodated religious ceremonies. Precisely what occurred during ceremonies in the avenue is not known, but it is easy to assume that religious processions took place between the stones. Evidence suggests that avenues were deeply connected to the stone circles of the Neolithic. This poses a mystery. Nobody knows what Neolithic stone circles were used for, other than the belief that they were used as religious enclosures. One fascinating similarity between the two is their tendency to align towards the solstice sun. Like many stone circle enclosures in Cumbria, Shap Avenue aligns towards the winter solstice sunrise, suggesting that events took place here at midwinter.

Shap Avenue is estimated to date to the Early Bronze Age. Like typical avenues of that period, Shap Avenue appears to be connected to several adjacent burial monuments. Skellaw Hill, a large round barrow near Shap Abbey, is believed by some to be the focal point for the avenue. Others draw attention to a far larger barrow, known as Shap Thorne to the south-east, a mound of stone topped by a large oak tree, making it visible for miles around.

– KEMP HOWE STONE CIRCLE –

Rev. James Simpson, a local antiquarian during the Victorian period, described an exceptionally large stone circle that once stood somewhere towards the centre of Shap Avenue. It was far larger than the other circles at Shap and was said to contain a single megalith at its centre. This circle, known as Carl Lofts, was removed in the eighteenth century to make way for ploughing, along with much of the avenue. The central stone was allegedly so large that seven gateposts were created after breaking it up into pieces.

– THE GOGGLEBY STONE –

There have also been numerous descriptions of the avenue over the centuries. The oldest comes courtesy of William Camden in his 1607 *Britannia*:

> *There be huge stones in forme of Pyramides, some 9 foote high and foureteene foot thicke, ranged directly as it were in a rowe for a mile in length .*

While there were certainly no pyramids here, this does match the description by James Simpson. Another account by William Stukeley in 1725 was extra detailed; his account reads as follows:

> *This avenue is seventy foot broad, composed of very large stones, set at equal intervals: it seems to be closed at this end [presumably describing Kemp Howe] ... Though its journey be northward, yet it makes a very large curve, or an arc of a circle, as those at Avebury.*

While today it is difficult to imagine what the avenue looked like, a few artistic representations had been created before and soon after its destruction. Lady

Lowther, of Lowther Estate, painted a watercolour of a colossal stone avenue in 1775. Although untitled, this painting presumably depicted Shap Avenue as it stood. Local Rev. James Simpson described the avenue as incomplete in the nineteenth century. Using previous sources, he created a detailed plan of the monument, and although its accuracy is questionable, it mostly depicted what previous antiquarians had described.

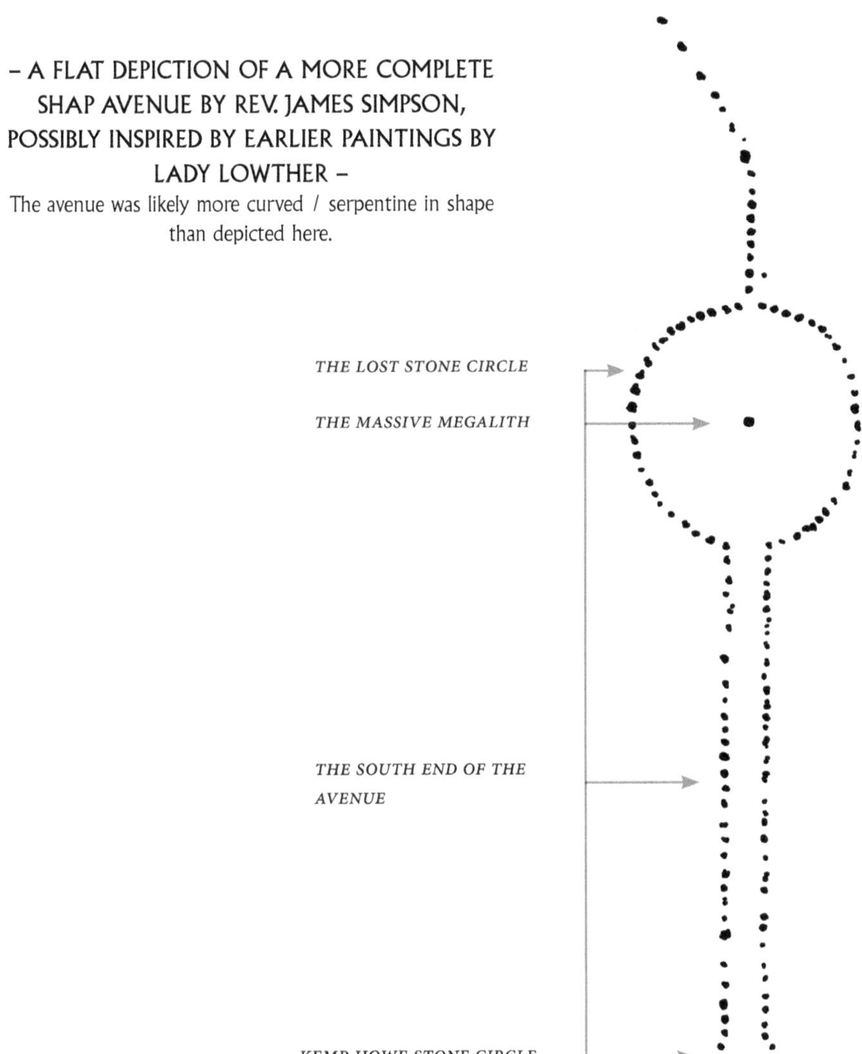

– A FLAT DEPICTION OF A MORE COMPLETE SHAP AVENUE BY REV. JAMES SIMPSON, POSSIBLY INSPIRED BY EARLIER PAINTINGS BY LADY LOWTHER –

The avenue was likely more curved / serpentine in shape than depicted here.

Despite the centuries of abuse, efforts have been made to restore Shap Avenue to some of its former glory. These days, the Goggleby Stone is easily the most outstanding stone of the avenue, but its prominence is only the result of a re-erection following its toppling in 1975. After several failed attempts to re-erect the Goggleby Stone in its original hole, a decision was made to hold it in place with a concrete base. If we put the ethics of this decision aside, it still begs the question: *If we could not erect this stone in 1975, how did people do it 4,500 years ago?*

From the Goggleby Stone, you can gaze north-west towards the Aspers Field Stone, another megalith secured in place with concrete. On its top is a deeply etched ring mark, the clearest example of such a motif in Cumbria. Unlike those found at Copt Howe, Grasmere or Patterdale, this cup and ring design does not share any distinct similarities to motifs found in Ireland. Generic carvings like this are far more prevalent to the east of the Pennines, in Yorkshire and Northumberland.

The question of how far – and in what direction – Shap Avenue led is still debated to this day. Shap Avenue possibly served as the spine from which all of Eastern Cumbria's monuments stem and may have once stretched for several miles. Possible directions include Gunnerkeld to the north or as far as Penrith. Some also argue in favour of Moor Divock being the destination since it sits north-west of Shap, the direction in which the avenue currently points.

Whatever the case, we can obviously understand one thing: Shap Avenue must have been immensely important to have warranted so much time and labour.

– WHITE RAISE ROUND CAIRN –

WHITE RAISE

White Raise is a Bronze Age round cairn situated on White Raise Pike, a small hill below Langhowe Pike to the west of Shap. Unfortunately, any views are obstructed, as White Raise sits snugly into a dip at the top of the hill. From adjacent peaks this would certainly make for an excellent marker to guide travellers towards Shap, although its use was clearly funerary.

Burial monuments like White Raise were built in Cumbria during the Bronze Age (2500–700 BC). Unlike the modern cairns that mark the fells across Cumbria, these ancient mausoleums are far larger in scale, easily identified by their bowl shape. White Raise is not a particularly large example of a round cairn; even with its top intact it would have only stood at around 6ft tall. Despite being only 2 miles from Shap Avenue, it is a rather lonely cairn, with only a few smaller burial monuments dotting the nearby hillside.

Rev. James Simpson was the first to excavate the cairn back in the nineteenth century. Simpson discovered charred bones and fragments of an urn 'scored

- AN UNCOVERED KERB CAIRN FOUND EN ROUTE TO THE ROUND CAIRN -

with parallel lines', plainly identifying it as a Bronze Age monument. He also noted that the stones of the cairn had been ravaged by locals to aid the building of dry-stone walls in the area, leaving the large hole we now see in its centre.

Round cairns are often confused for directional markers for walkers and farmers, which may have caused unnecessary damage in the past. We can safely assume that many round cairns (most dating to the Bronze Age) were plundered to build dry stone walls, as the abundance of easily accessible stone would have been tempting to farmers in centuries passed.

CROSBY RAVENSWORTH

The Crosby Ravensworth Stone Circles are found scattered across the moorland between the villages of Shap and Crosby Ravensworth. A favourite spot for local dog walkers, this tract of land comes highly recommended for anyone seeking a pleasant walk in the countryside. The views across to the Lake District's eastern fells, as well as the Pennines to the east, are among the nicest listed in this book.

Almost every stone circle makes use of pink granite and, curiously, each one includes a single stone of a different variety. Several stone circles of an uncommonly small size also survive here – suggesting a practical reason for circles so small to exist on this stretch of land. Why these unusual circles are present here has been the subject of much debate, making this an ideal area for a walk with friends with similar interests. Throughout the author's countless trips to this moor, not one has been without enjoyable speculation on the area's purpose in prehistoric times.

Most of the Crosby Ravensworth circles appear to have been strongly linked with prehistoric funerals. What we find here is a Neolithic and Early Bronze Age crematorium and cemetery, similar in plan to coastal landscapes like Burnmoor or Lacra Bank. Unfortunately, the monuments here have received several careless antiquarian excavations, requiring us to rely on the work of curious Victorians to piece together an understanding of these curious sites.

– CROSBY RAVENSWORTH –

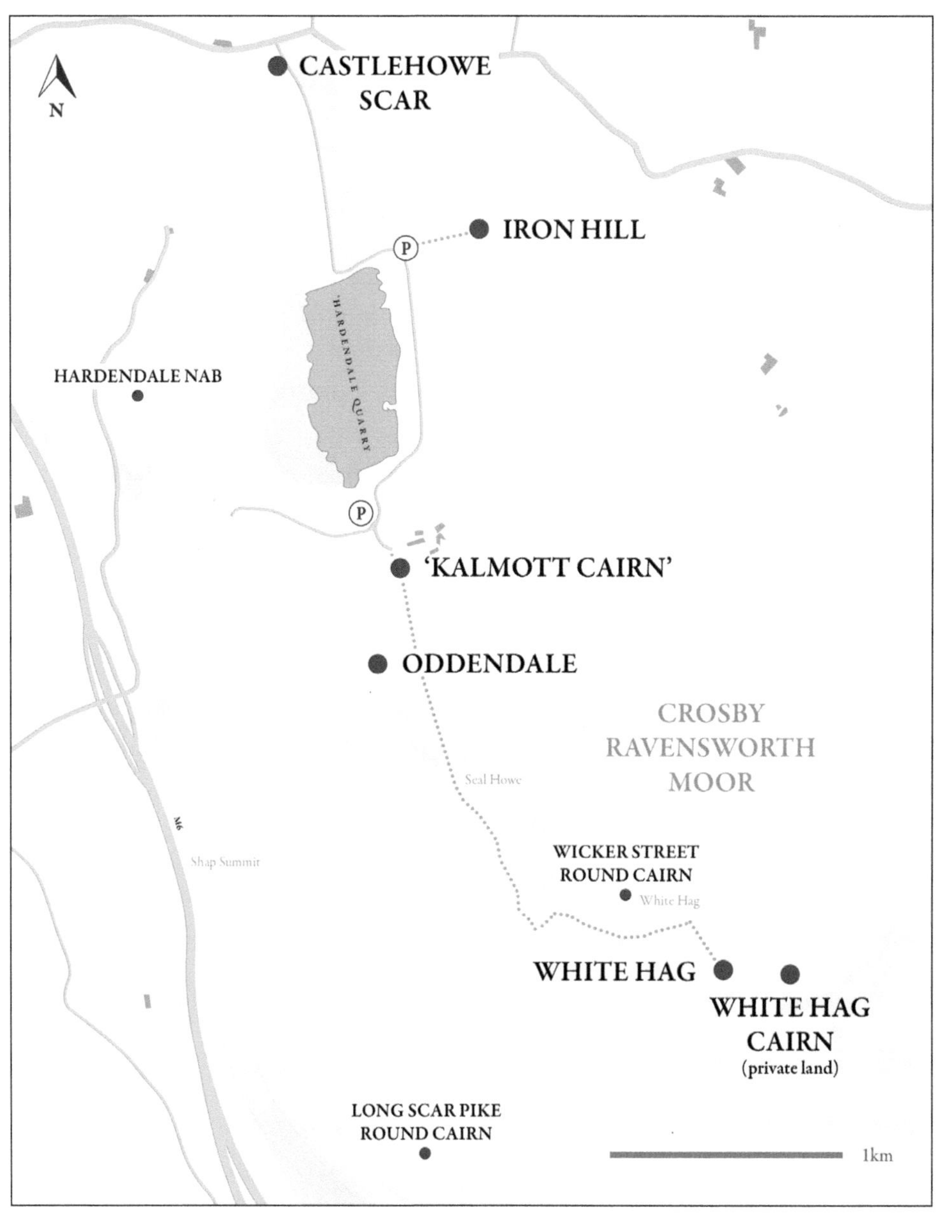

ODDENDALE STONE CIRCLE

A handsome stone circle with a few peculiar features, Oddendale comes with a litany of excavation details to help us understand its purpose. Finding the circle can be difficult, as its position at the brow of a hill makes spotting it from a distance a challenge. Nevertheless, it is only a short walk from a major footpath and can be easily navigated to using a map.

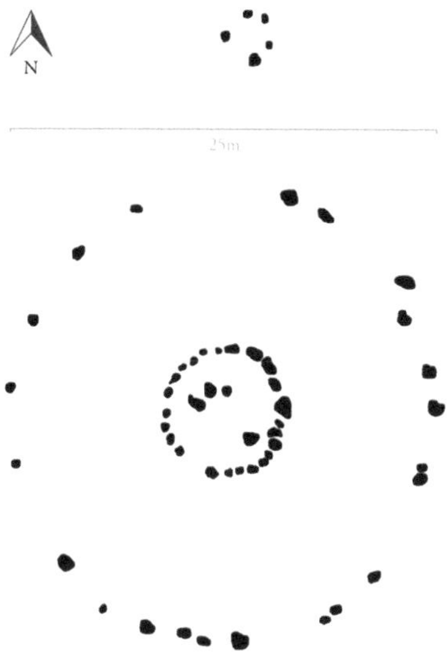

Oddendale comprises two near perfectly round circles, one set concentrically within the other. The outer circle consists of thirty-four pink granite stones; the inner circle was created using twenty-three stones of the same variety. At the north end of the outer

– ODDENDALE STONE CIRCLE FROM ABOVE –

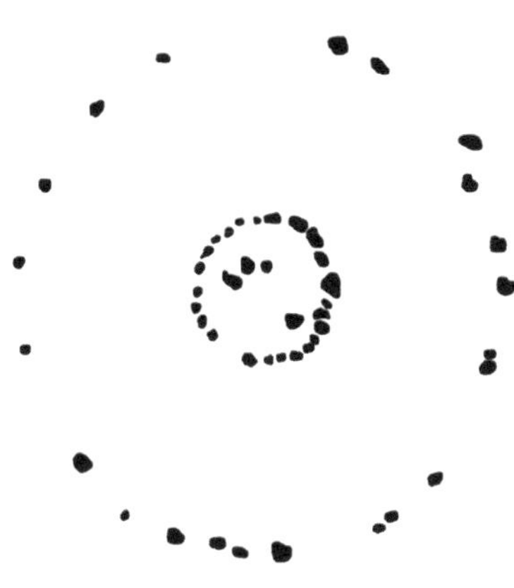

– ODDENDALE STONE CIRCLE'S OUTER CIRCLE IN WINTER –

circle is a secondary satellite circle, the remaining stones of a kerb cairn which has been ransacked.

The inner circle serves as a kerb around a massive cairn, a style of burial dating to the Early Bronze Age. Practically all concentric stone circles found across Cumbria contain kerb cairns, so we may assume they were always designed to mark graves. However, as is typical of Early Bronze Age stone circles, Oddendale is likely the final stage of an ever-evolving monument. Archaeologists P. Turnbull and D. Walsh carried out a modern excavation at an adjacent circle in 1990, prior to its destruction by the nearby quarry. This would lead the archaeologists to conclude the nearby site was created in four phases, with centuries separating each stage.

The first phase, likely dating to the Neolithic, consisted of twenty-four oak posts erected into a concentric arrangement, each topped by Stonehenge-esque lintels. Assuming the builders were creatively motivated, we can imagine that these posts were decorated to an extent, either carved or painted. During the second phase these oak posts were removed, and the pits filled with pink granite stones, much like the Oddendale Stone Circle we see today.

The third phase involved cobbling the area between the inner and outer circles to create a ring cairn, in a remarkably similar fashion to Birkrigg. Deeper into this layer, a whole human skeleton was discovered, buried within the centre of the inner circle in a foetal position. Alongside this skeleton was the shard of a bell beaker. Human bones, fragments of pottery and flint knives were also found inside the inner circle, which all likely dated to this phase.

During stage four, a rectangular platform was added to the outer edge of the inner circle, created using several massive slab-like stones. This was placed at the south-west corner of the circle, possibly aligning the monument towards the winter solstice sunset. Numerous fragments of unburnt bone were found on top of the platform, indicating that bones had been intentionally pulverised here.

The obvious question is: *why?*

As grotesque as it may sound, the platform may have been an area used to strip bodies of flesh before cremation, typically by being left to the elements. This practice, known as excarnation, is known to have been performed at wooden circles across England. For instance, the Sanctuary, a wooden circle south of Avebury (Britain's largest stone circle), is also believed to have been the site of excarnations. This was possibly a ritualistic process, but not one without necessity. During the Bronze Age, cremations would have been performed using wood fires, and so time and resources could be saved via excarnation.

To summarise: Oddendale was clearly an area with strong ties to funeral ceremonies. Not only were there numerous cremations taking place within its centre, but whole bodies dating to the Early Bronze Age were unearthed from within it. A likely scenario is that concentric stone circles like Oddendale enclosed cremations within their inner circle, while allowing spectators to occupy their outer circle. During the Neolithic, concentric circles were made from wood, simply enclosing excarnations and cremations. Later in the Early Bronze Age, these sites were converted into kerb cairns, where several eminent people were buried. While this may be true for Oddendale, this was not necessarily the case for all concentric circles.

Perhaps more fascinating than the excavation itself are the possibilities it presents. Numerous prehistoric sites across northern England, and especially Cumbria, have yet to be as thoroughly studied as Oddendale. Perhaps, if modern excavations were carried out at sites such as Swinside, Castlerigg, Shap Avenue, Brat's Hill, or Casterton, we could begin to piece together a similarly exciting timeline.

CASTLEHOWE SCAR

Castlehowe Scar is the most northernly stone circle on Crosby Ravensworth moor. It sits in a small field next to the junction towards Hardendale Quarry. Found on private land, you will need to either seek permission from the landowners, or peek over the nearby wall to view the circle without trespassing.

Two rows of stones, five in each row, are capped off by a single boulder. While it is not immediately apparent, Castlehowe Scar is not technically a circle, but rather a stone square, both sides aligning towards the south-east. If this was an intentional design choice then Castlehowe Scar is aligned with the winter solstice sunrise, an alignment found repeatedly among prehistoric sites in Cumbria (Shap Avenue and Swinside for instance).

While Castlehowe Scar's small size would usually imply that it was a burial marker, no burial cairn sits within its centre. It is also unlikely that gatherings were taking place within an enclosure this small, suggesting that it was used for neither burials nor religious gatherings. Instead, Castlehowe Scar seems to have more in common with a circle known as Leacet Hill, just south-east of Penrith.

– CASTLEHOWE SCAR –

Leacet Hill was excavated in the early twentieth century, revealing that it was used as a funeral pyre during the Early Bronze Age.

Along burial landscapes like Crosby Ravensworth, it is likely that a number of these ancient crematoriums would have been needed. Castlehowe Scar was possibly an example of such a crematorium, though there is little evidence for this aside from comparison. The truth is: nobody knows exactly what Castlehowe Scar was used for, and modern questions will require modern excavations to answer.

– CASTLEHOWE SCAR FROM ABOVE –

A lone granite bluestone lies at the southern tip of the monument, which is the only stone that has been sculpted to shape using tools. This is a common feature in Eastern Cumbria, but especially on Crosby Ravensworth Moor, where every circle includes a single stone of a different shape or rock strata. Some believe that these stones were used like crosshairs, aligning the circles to specific points in the landscape. Others have suggested that different coloured stones represent the worlds of the living and the dead. These theories are, of course, just speculation. The choice to use a different variety of stone may have been simply aesthetic or purely arbitrary. Pink granite boulders can be found scattered all over Eastern Cumbria, and the choice to use them could have been due to their prevalence.

IRON HILL

Opposite Hardendale Quarry, on Iron Hill, sit two disfigured stone circles. They lie beside a footpath that cuts straight up the side of the hill, hugging a wall to the east of the quarry. Once you arrive at the crest of the hill, you can follow the wall all the way to the circles.

Iron Hill North sits at the base of a mound, which is the disfigured remains of a bowl barrow: a burial mound resembling an upturned bowl. A wall was built straight through the centre of the barrow in the nineteenth century, and half the stones were illegally removed by a landowner in the mid 1980s.

Iron Hill South is also the remains of a bowl barrow, the stones simply being a kerb to keep the mound neatly raised. In this respect, the bowl barrows on Iron Hill are comparable to kerb cairns (such as Boot Kerb Cairn, pictured on the front cover of this book), only on a far larger scale.

The bowl barrows on Iron Hill were the focus of antiquarian investigations during the Victorian era, when artifacts indicative of both the Neolithic and Bronze Age were discovered. Iron Hill South had human remains and animal bone tools buried within its centre, probably dating from the Neolithic period. The same excavation, paradoxically, unearthed a Bronze Age dagger from

– IRON HILL NORTH –

– IRON HILL SOUTH –

between the two circles. The combination of Neolithic and Bronze Age artifacts is possibly an indicator that this was an Early Bronze Age site, created towards the end of the Neolithic period.

Iron Hill South is also known to have been looted in the Victorian Period, judging by this rather unnerving account by antiquarian John S. Blandin in 1860:

> *It was carelessly opened a few years ago, and in the south-west side was found a human skeleton of gigantic proportions.*

People don't tend to gloss over the skeleton of a giant, so it is assumed that this description was simply an exaggeration by Blandin. No cremated remains or Bronze Age artifacts were uncovered inside Iron Hill South. Instead, only the skeletons of the dead and crude tools made from animal bones were found. Such burial customs are also seen at Levens Park and Burnmoor, Early Bronze Age sites deeply connected to funerary ceremonies.

– IRON HILL NORTH FROM ABOVE –

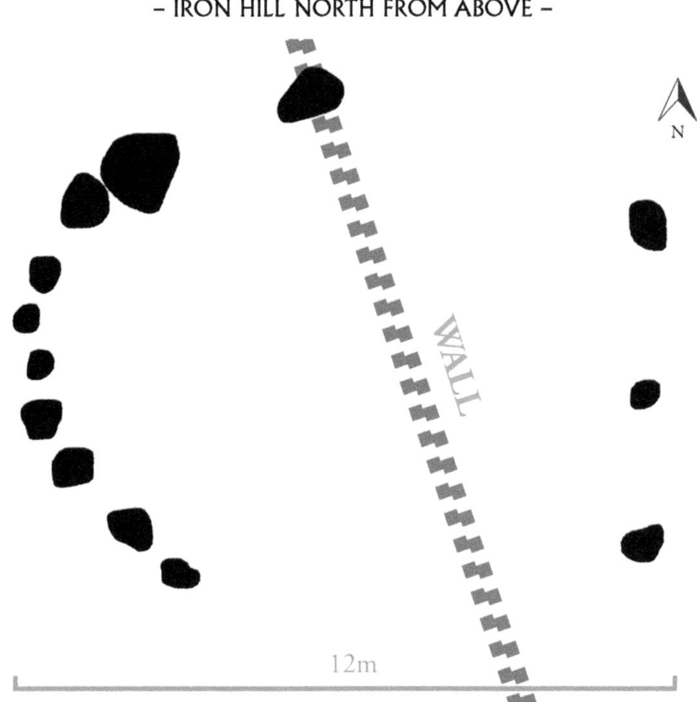

WHITE HAG

White Hag Stone Circle sits in a bleak field at the south-east corner of the Crosby Ravensworth Moor, just down from the craggy peak of White Hag. Several paths lead south from Iron Hill and Oddendale towards White Hag, yet it will require a small venture off the path to see it.

White Hag consists of eleven pink granite boulders, which are difficult to see throughout most of the year due to the long moorland grass. It is a similar shape and size to Castlehowe Scar and was likewise possibly used as a cremation pyre during the Early Bronze Age. White Hag, however, has received even less study, and again, there have been no known excavations at the site.

A double-humped round cairn, known as White Hag Cairn, sits in the field below the stone circle. It was perhaps the final resting place for those who were cremated within the nearby circle, although only an excavation could confirm this. Despite there being no known excavations at the cairn, there is a clear trench that cuts through its centre. The sad truth is that looters are probably to blame for this, having dug in search of treasures, or possibly even giant skeletons.

- WHITE HAG ROUND CAIRN -

MOOR DIVOCK

Moor Divock is a sloping tract of moorland, stretching 3km between Pooley Bridge and Askham. Its position at the tail end of the High Street Roman road and its views over Ullswater make it a popular area for hikers and casual walkers alike. Besides the sheep and farmers that work the land, this rugged moor has sat relatively undisturbed for millennia, as have the Bronze Age monuments found within it. Moor Divock contains an Early Bronze Age complex akin to Burnmoor and Crosby Ravensworth, an area home to countless burial cairns, enclosures and stone circles.

The regions containing Castlerigg, Shap Avenue, Langdale and Long Meg are all within sight of Moor Divock. It is often debated whether the complex of prehistoric monuments here was connected in any way to the monuments at Shap in particular, since the village is easily spotted to the east. Although this could be the case, the prehistoric monuments occupying Moor Divock could be as easily connected to those at Penrith, the North Lake District or Grasmere. For this reason, it is probably best to view Moor Divock as a separate entity. Essentially, this attractive little moor is sandwiched between some of Cumbria's largest prehistoric sites, and an excellent area to gain a panoramic perspective of an ancient landscape.

For those seeking a ramble, a walk in the countryside with the supplement of stunning views and historical monuments, Moor Divock is among the most pleasant areas to do so in Cumbria. Rarely can you find such a well-presented collection of prehistoric monuments, some understood, others mysterious and elusive in their purpose. This is a piece of land so brilliantly independent, so robust in its character, so unapologetic of its colourful history, that less than justice would be done by bypassing it in favour of more eye-catching regions across Cumbria.

– MOOR DIVOCK –

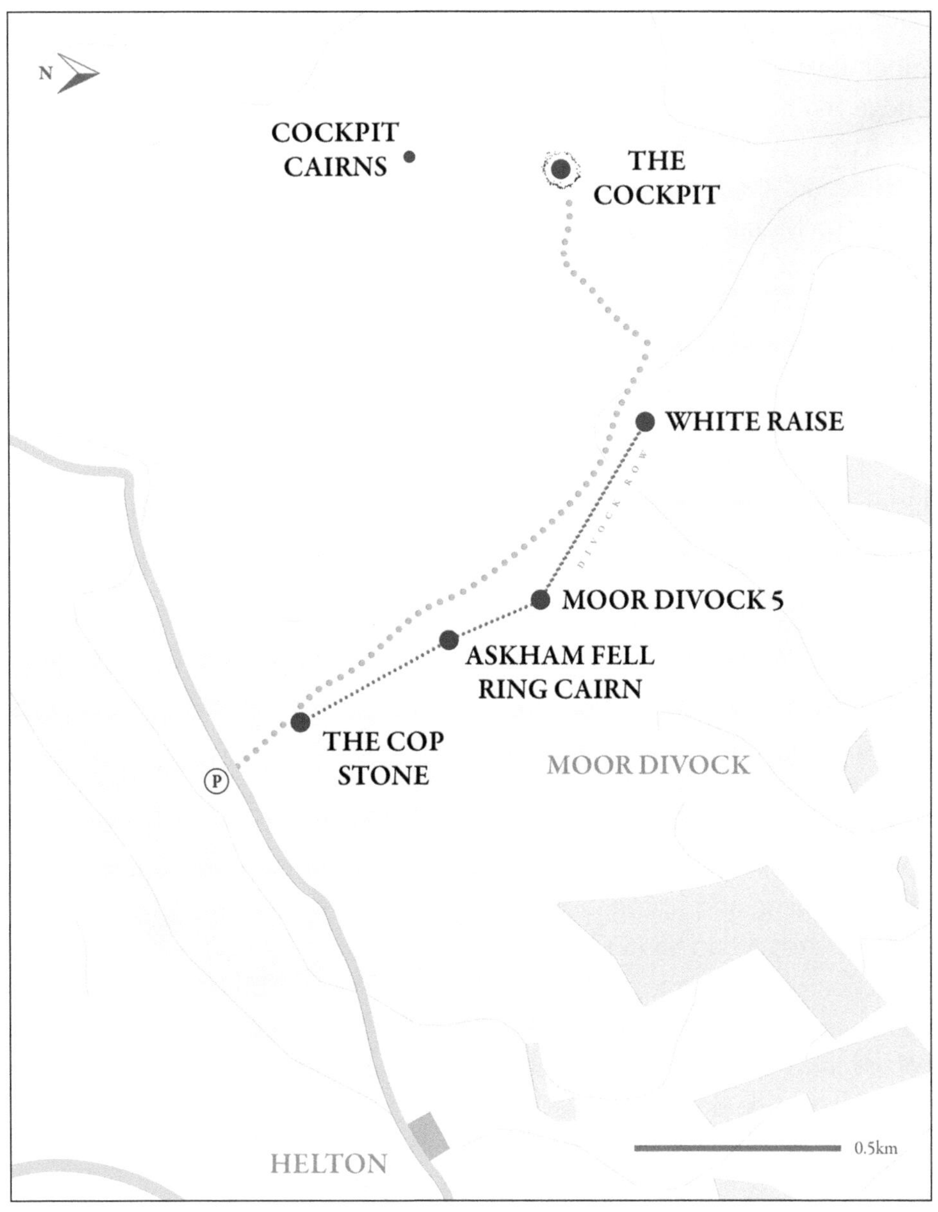
N
COCKPIT
CAIRNS
THE
COCKPIT
WHITE RAISE
DIVOCK ROW
MOOR DIVOCK 5
ASKHAM FELL
RING CAIRN
THE COP
STONE
MOOR DIVOCK
P
HELTON
0.5km

DIVOCK AVENUE

Divock Avenue stretches for 1 mile south-east across Moor Divock. It is a double row of small stones, each placed around 7m apart. The avenue is difficult to see during the summer due to the thick moorland bracken, so it is far easier to appreciate during the colder months. Even then, most of the smaller stones have become buried over time, and sinkholes that pockmark the moor have swallowed whole portions of the avenue.

Despite Divock Avenue's rough shape, following its proposed path will still lead you from site to site, acting as a guide between Moor Divock's prehistoric monuments. It forms a line 110m past several burial monuments, providing evidence that Divock Avenue was perhaps a path through which funeral precessions were performed. This is a theory like that proposed for the stone avenue at Lacra Bank, a ceremonial path used to cremate and honour the dead (not unlike the aisle of a church or parade ground).

– DIVOCK 5 –
(Askham Fell Ring Cairn in the background)

Divock 5 is just one of the many round cairns found on Moor Divock, and was built at the centre of the avenue. This otherwise unassuming cairn has three square megaliths sprouting from its top, which form the most prominent section of the avenue. An urn was unearthed from the cairn during an excavation in the nineteenth century, implying that the cairn dates to the Bronze Age. Despite being found within a round cairn, the urn's position at the centre of the avenue is curious. A similar urn was unearthed at Lacra Avenue, which was believed to be a later burial. In this case, however, the cairn at Divock 5 was built underneath the avenue, implying that the urn burial possibly predated Divock Avenue.

– DIVOCK AVENUE AS DIAGRAMMED BY M. WAISTELL TAYLOR IN 1885 –

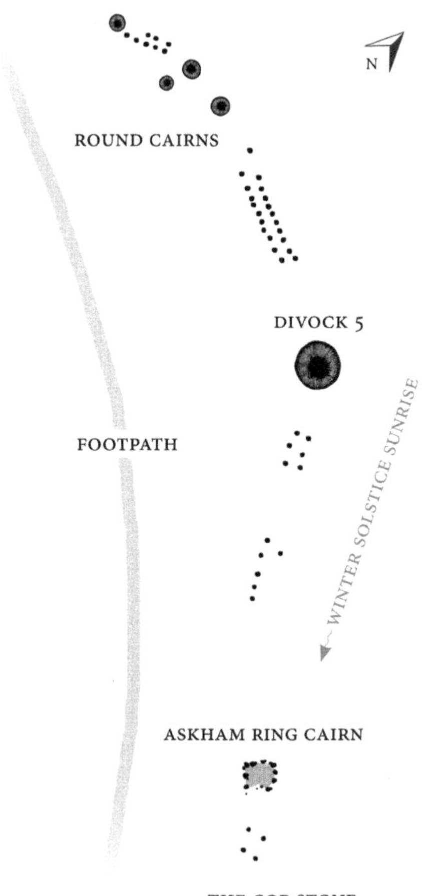

Author's Notes: The avenue points to the north-west / south-east, a common alignment in Cumbria. Sites that point in a similar direction, such as Shap Avenue, have been linked to the winter solstice sunrise. This, of course, is just a theory. There will never be any concrete evidence to back up the claims of solar alignments, so why not witness it and decide for yourself?

THE COP STONE

The Cop Stone is the first megalith you will encounter on the trail across Moor Divock if heading north-west from Helton. From here you can gaze northward and observe the numerous lumps in the landscape that make up the Cockpit Round Barrow Cemetery, a field full of burial cairns adjacent to Divock Avenue.

This leaning megalith is just the sole remaining stone of a damaged ring cairn, a low circle of stones surrounding a burial or pit. Although the ring cairn is now barely visible, this megalith is proof of a rather showy burial enclosure that once stood here.

Surveying your surroundings from the Cop Stone, it is easy to see that Moor Divock is not only an obvious place for thoroughfare between the Lake District and Eastern Cumbria, but also an excellent vantage point to see across Shap Avenue. Even now you can look out onto the valley below, and picture what an amazing sight this landscape would have been during the Bronze Age.

– THE COP STONE –

ASKHAM FELL RING CAIRN

Askham Fell Ring Cairn sits on a raised mound around 0.5km north-west of the Cop Stone. It is located at the centre of the moor, and it will usually be the first stone circle you will spot along Divock Avenue if you head north-west from Helton, thanks to its prominence.

Ring cairns are relatively rare in England, and this is an especially well-preserved and exaggerated example. Askham Fell Ring Cairn was constructed using ten boulders, which form a small rectangular enclosure atop a ring of stone. The monument stands only 2ft tall and is easily inspected from ground level.

Perhaps the most unusual feature of the cairn is the ring of stone, on which the enclosure sits. This is the eponymous ring cairn of the monument, but it has more the appearance of a modified round cairn. Thanks to the work of antiquarians, we can piece together a rough idea of this peculiar monument's purpose.

Excavations in 1866 uncovered a layer of sand buried inside the centre of the cairn, on top of which fragments of pottery and a bowl were unearthed. Digging deeper, further cremated remains were found at lower levels, suggesting that this pit had been used for the purpose of cremations on numerous occasions.

Ring cairns are only loosely defined monuments, without a strict blueprint from which to compare between each cairn. They often contain buried human remains, and therefore it is assumed they were used during funerals. Since all examples are different, it would be dishonest to say we fully understand the purpose of these mysterious stone rings. While defined as a ring cairn in almost all descriptions of Moor Divock, Askham Fell Ring Cairn has more in common with small burial circles such as Grey Croft.

WHITE RAISE

White Raise is an iconic burial cairn constructed at the end of Divock Avenue, which is not to be confused with the round cairn of the same name west of Shap. White Raise is a round cairn, a massive mound of stones dating to the Bronze Age. As mentioned previously, these monuments usually covered multiple urn and cist burials. This is perhaps the most excellent example of such a monument in northern England, with several archetypical features on full display.

An excavation in 1860 discovered a cist within the cairn covered by a large capstone. This can still be seen today, representing the clearest example of a cist in Cumbria. After it was pried open, this ancient coffin was found to contain the body of a single adult male, buried in a crouched position. Being in such a position meant that the man had his knees pushed up to his chest and arms tucked up to his face. This implies that he had been tightly packed into the small cist, almost completely filling its space, a style of burial common in the Early Bronze Age.

Curiously, the cist was not found at the centre of the cairn, instead sitting a metre to the west, indicating that there are multiple burials hidden within White

Raise. Unlike the countless small cairns scattered across the moor, this massive cairn was clearly intended to hold the remains of several people, similar in purpose to Dunmail Raise and Brownthwaite Pike.

– WHITE RAISE ROUND CAIRN'S WELL-PRESERVED CIST –

White Raise is a moderately sized round cairn compared to others found in Cumbria. However, it is far larger in size when compared to other round cairns on Moor Divock. This implies that it was of a higher importance to those burying their dead here, and its position at the northern end of Divock Avenue suggests that only distinguished members of society were buried within it.

If you climb to the top of the cairn, the feeling of being above your surroundings is immediately clear. From here you can look down Divock Avenue and witness the winter solstice sunrise over the Cop Stone. Every winter solstice sunrise, the sun's rays would beam between the stones of the avenue, directing one's gaze towards White Raise and those buried within it.

While this book only highlights the key round cairns in Cumbria, there were countless examples built across the fells of the Lake District. In upland areas it is common to find round cairns that are made of stone. In lowland areas they are usually constructed of earth and known as round barrows. White Raise is a near perfect example of this upland tradition that has its burial cist exposed for all to see.

THE COCKPIT

The Cockpit is an unusual stone circle at the northern end of Moor Divock. It is located north-west of Divock Avenue, occupying an elevated position overlooking the moor. Looking to the west from here allows views all the way over Ullswater, making this a particularly scenic site to visit.

High Street Roman road runs adjacent to the Cockpit, and you can often find intrepid hikers using it as a rest stop. Tourist information often explains how the Cockpit was likely 'a place to congregate after a long journey over the fells'. After all, High Street possibly follows a prehistoric path, and travellers over the moor could have rested and traded within the Cockpit. Excavations have revealed a particularly complex history at the Cockpit though, and the original purpose of the enclosure remains a mystery. It is not an easily assessed site as no comparable stone circles exist in Cumbria.

A double circle of stones encases a cobbled ring, which is mostly covered with soil and grass. The larger stones that make the monument so prominent seem to only serve as the kerb for this ring of loose cobbles. Some areas appear to have piles of stone dumped onto them. These were probably clearance cairns from Middle Bronze Age agriculture, showing a possible disregard for the monument during that period.

The stones originally sat on top of a bank of earth, which has degraded over time, causing most of the stones to topple. Research has shown that the Cockpit was constructed by backfilling a trench in which the stones were placed. First a circular trench was dug, into which two rings of stones were positioned. The earth was then back filled, leaving the stones elevated and shallowly buried. After this, the cobbling was added between the rings, creating the thick band of stones we see today.

Why this was done is a mystery, although there are several theories. The lack of large natural boulders on Moor Divock could have been a reason to build with smaller stones. However, perhaps more credible is the idea that the Cockpit is not a stone circle at all, but instead a ring cairn. Two prominent burial cairns were built into the sides of the circle, indicating that the Cockpit's embankment was possibly seen as a form of burial cairn. So, was the Cockpit a ring cairn?

The answer is complicated. Archaeological evidence indicates that funeral ceremonies took place at the majority of ring cairns across Britain. This does not necessarily prove that they were primarily built to inter the dead. Instead, it only suggests that people used them during funerals. Even in the modern day, our religious centres, such as churches or mosques, are used for both worship and wedding ceremonies and funerals, but never just a single function.

Perhaps the only comparable monument is Levens Park Ring Cairn, a kerbed ring of cobblestones incorporating several burial cairns into its circumference. Ring cairns are thought to have been used as an alternative to stone circle enclosures in some regions, but some were converted to burial monuments during the Bronze Age.

Nonetheless, the age of the burials within the circle remains a mystery. No modern excavations have taken place within the Cockpit, so there is insufficient evidence to indicate whether they are contemporary with the circle or not. The age of the circle is not known, and it could be argued that the Cockpit dates as far back as the Neolithic period.

– THE COCKPIT STONE CIRCLE AND EMBANKMENT AS SURVEYED BY M. WAISTELL TAYLOR IN 1885 –

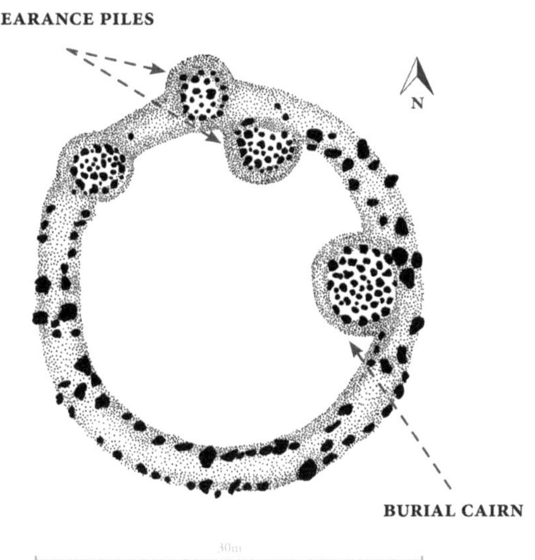

Conjecture notwithstanding, the purpose of the Cockpit is still debated, and researchers do not know when or why it was constructed. It is by far the most notable manmade feature on Moor Divock, deserving of the upmost study.

Author's Notes: To summarise, the Cockpit is a particularly difficult site to research. Hardly any archaeological evidence points to a specific date of construction, and the circle's unique shape avoids direct comparisons. While the idea that the Cockpit was a religious enclosure of some variety is the most popular theory put forth in tourist literature, its purpose is almost always neglected mention. If we are to use circumstantial evidence alone, the Cockpit is likely an Early Bronze Age funerary monument, not unlike the other circles on Moor Divock.

KNIPE SCAR

The landscape immediately north of Shap is best known for its large gravel quarries and the M6 motorway. North Shap is not an area typically regarded as scenic, thanks to the presence of these eyesores. However, with a walk in the right direction, it should become apparent that this was once one of Cumbria's most wonderful megalithic hotspots.

The most beneficial vantage point just north of Shap is Knipe Scar, a 340m-high limestone outcrop between Moor Divock and Shap Avenue. It is a wonderful place to get a perspective on the eastern edge of the Lake District, with clear views as far as High Street and Haweswater. It was on Knipe Scar that several Bronze Age burial monuments were built, possibly due to the hill's breathtaking views.

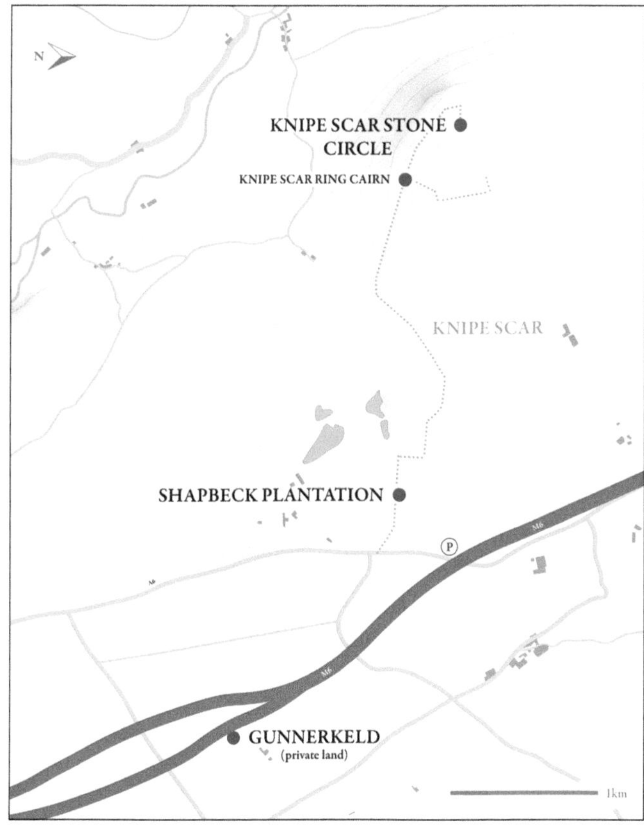

GUNNERKELD

Heading southbound on the M6 past Shap, you can catch a fleeting glimpse of Gunnerkeld Stone Circle. Sitting in a private field just off the east side of the M6, its proximity to the motorway has deterred visitors for decades. Despite this, Gunnerkeld's grandeur cannot be overstated. This is, perhaps, northern England's finest concentric stone circle, and the largest example of such a circle in Cumbria.

Nearly every stone has toppled, with the notable exceptions being the two tall megaliths making up the circle's north entrance. The outer ring is made up of nineteen large pink granite stones, while the inner circle makes up the majority with thirty-one stones. As far back as AD 1577, William Camden mentioned Gunnerkeld in his survey, *Britannia*. It seems that even in the sixteenth century the circle was in a state of ruin. Camden noted that, 'The injury of Time has put Gunnerkeld beyond all possibility of pointing out the date of construction.'

– GUNNERKELD'S INNER STONE CIRCLE –

An entranceway can be found on the northern edge, similar in style to the entrance at Castlerigg. This possibly demonstrates a basic understanding of orientation to the cardinal points. Another similarity to Castlerigg is the square enclosure, a rectangular arrangement of stones erected within Gunnerkeld's inner circle. These similarities could suggest that Gunnerkeld was built within memory of Castlerigg's construction, possibly in the Neolithic period.

– GUNNERKELD FROM ABOVE –

GREEN: SOUTH WEST STONES
BLUE: 'INNER CHAMBER'
RED: PORTAL STONES

N

Like Oddendale, the inner circle contains a burial cist. Because all examples of concentric stone circles found in Cumbria contain burials, it is possible that the inner circle is nothing more than a grandiose kerb cairn. This again raises the question: were concentric circles created for religious gatherings, or were they simply funerary in purpose? Gunnerkeld's large diameter suggests it was a religious enclosure (similar in form to Castlerigg). But without excavations, there is no way to know in what order the key elements of the site were erected.

Jean Scott-Smith, vice chairman of the Shap Local History Society, believes that while Gunnerkeld sits outside Shap Avenue's path, it may have been connected. The northerly portion of Shap Avenue has been lost for all recorded history, and there has never been any confirmation on where it led. Scott-Smith considers that Shap Avenue may have divided and led eastwards towards Gunnerkeld. If this was the case, then why?

The answer may be connected to what Shap Avenue was following. Scott-Smith believes that this may have been water. She notes that Shap Avenue seems to

– GUNNERKELD'S ENTRANCEWAY –

follow natural springs. Once upon a time, the springs surrounding Shap were particularly forceful, occasionally gushing like geysers during rainy spells. Translating 'Gunnerkeld' from old Norse reveals the site was once known as 'Gunnar's Spring', implying that a natural spring once existed here, a resource of vital importance during prehistory.

Neolithic axe heads are often found close to water, such as the Irish Sea. As explained in Chapter 1, Langdale axes may have been buried close to water sources as offerings. Water is a source of life, whether it is to drink or to cultivate crops. Witnessing water gushing from the ground may have appeared like a miracle, and would surely not have gone unnoticed to the heavily religious culture of the Neolithic. Plausibly, this could have inspired the creation of a religious enclosure.

The scale of the outer circle and its proximity to a natural spring certainly suggests that Gunnerkeld was a Neolithic religious enclosure, in a similar vein to Castlerigg or Swinside. To a culture who venerated their landscape, land next to such an active spring would have undoubtedly been consecrated ground. If this was the case, then we can assume Gunnerkeld was converted into its current concentric form during the Bronze Age period.

This is not the only stone circle to be found next to flowing water. Antiquarians often noted that stone circles were created near springs (Elva Plain and Swinside, for instance). Of course, this may be explained with simple practicalities. If a society were large enough to construct megalithic monuments, they would have needed a flowing source of water nearby to survive. For this reason, any theory associating water to religious beliefs should perhaps be taken with a grain of salt, and not as indisputable fact.

SHAPBECK

This dilapidated concentric stone circle sits next to Shapbeck Plantation, at the southern edge of Knipe Scar. It is a recent rediscovery, and from how it looks, a sad state of affairs. Shapbeck comprises three concentric rings of stone, the only concentric circle in Cumbria to contain more than two stone circles. There are fifty-three stones in total, but they are incredibly hard to see due to the site's current overgrown state.

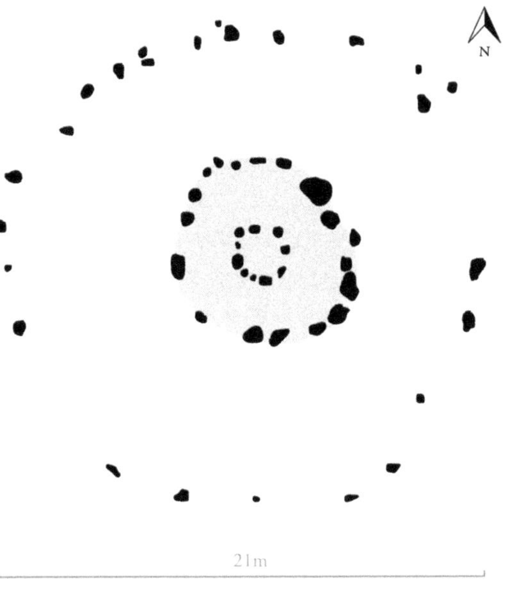

Shapbeck draws parallels to other concentric stone circles in Cumbria, particularly Oddendale at Crosby Ravensworth. Like at Oddendale, the complexity of Shapbeck suggests it is only the final stage of an ever-evolving monument. Cobblestones fill the area between the inner and middle circles, which are possibly the remains of a ring cairn, an Early Bronze Age monument. The innermost circle is also possibly Early Bronze Age, being a kerb cairn like those found at Oddendale and Burnmoor. However, as seen repeatedly, at Oddendale, Gunnerkeld and Birkrigg, concentric stone circles were typically built on Neolithic foundations.

Shapbeck was excavated in 1883 by Shap's local antiquarian, Rev. James Simpson. He found a large, flat stone within the centre of the circle, on top of which 'areas of burning' were discovered. We can assume cremations were taking place within the inner circle. This again draws parallels to other concentric circles, especially Oddendale. If we were to speculate, we could assume that Shapbeck, like Oddendale, began its life as a wooden circle used to excarnate and cremate the dead, later becoming a ring cairn, and finally a concentric stone circle.

Author's Notes: While this site is fascinating, its state of ruin can make it a frustrating visit. There has also been a large pile of rubble dumped onto the north side of the circle, and the whole monument is covered in nettles and brambles.

KNIPE SCAR STONE CIRCLE

Knipe Scar Stone Circle is just one of many prehistoric sites along Knipe Scar's northern crag. The circle sits at the centre of the hilltop between the tall wall to the east and the cliff face to the west. It will require a modern excavation and some restoration work to fully understand. For now, only a few theories have been proposed on Knipe Scar's origins and purpose.

- THE CENTRAL STONE OF KNIPE SCAR STONE CIRCLE -

A ring of loose stones surrounds a central limestone megalith. Of all the stones that make up the circle, only the central stone is clearly defined enough to identify. As with most loosely defined monuments of this type, researchers have theorised that Knipe Scar Stone Circle is the remains of a ring cairn. If this is the case, then it may have been used as a religious enclosure for cremations and burials during the Early Bronze Age.

A clearly defined ring cairn can be found 500m to the south-east of the circle, and a bowl barrow sits 300m to the east. The presence of these monuments strongly suggests that those who built this enclosure were well versed in the construction of ring cairns. However, no ring cairns in Cumbria contain a central stone like this example. It instead bears a greater resemblance to Lacra D, a burial circle linked to a stone avenue. Some believe that the central stone at Lacra D is a monumental cap stone of a burial chamber (or cist), which may also be the case at Knipe Scar. Without further investigations there is no way to know for certain.

Author's Notes: Knipe Scar Stone Circle was easily the most underwhelming site ventured to while obtaining photographs for this field guide. Its overgrown state has rendered it practi cally invisible, and the lack of context behind its origins is frustrating. The circle does not come recommended, but the walk to access it can certainly be enjoyable.

ASBY SCAR

Asby Scar is a limestone pavement rising from the centre of the Eden Valley, allowing for commanding views across both the Lake District Fells and the Pennines.

A landscape enveloped in history, containing both Roman and Anglo-Saxon ruins, many artefacts originating from Asby Scar are now displayed across the world as priceless relics. It was on Asby Scar, in fact, that the famous Crosby Garret Helmet was discovered by a metal detectorist in 2010. At the summit of the hill is the Romano-British Castle Folds, a defended settlement built at the centre of Asby Scar.

Even though the region is best known for these Roman ruins, several megalithic monuments can be found scattered along the base of the hill, which are thought to date to a far earlier period. These are not believed to be directly connected to the predominantly Bronze Age megaliths at Shap but are instead thought to date to the earlier Neolithic period.

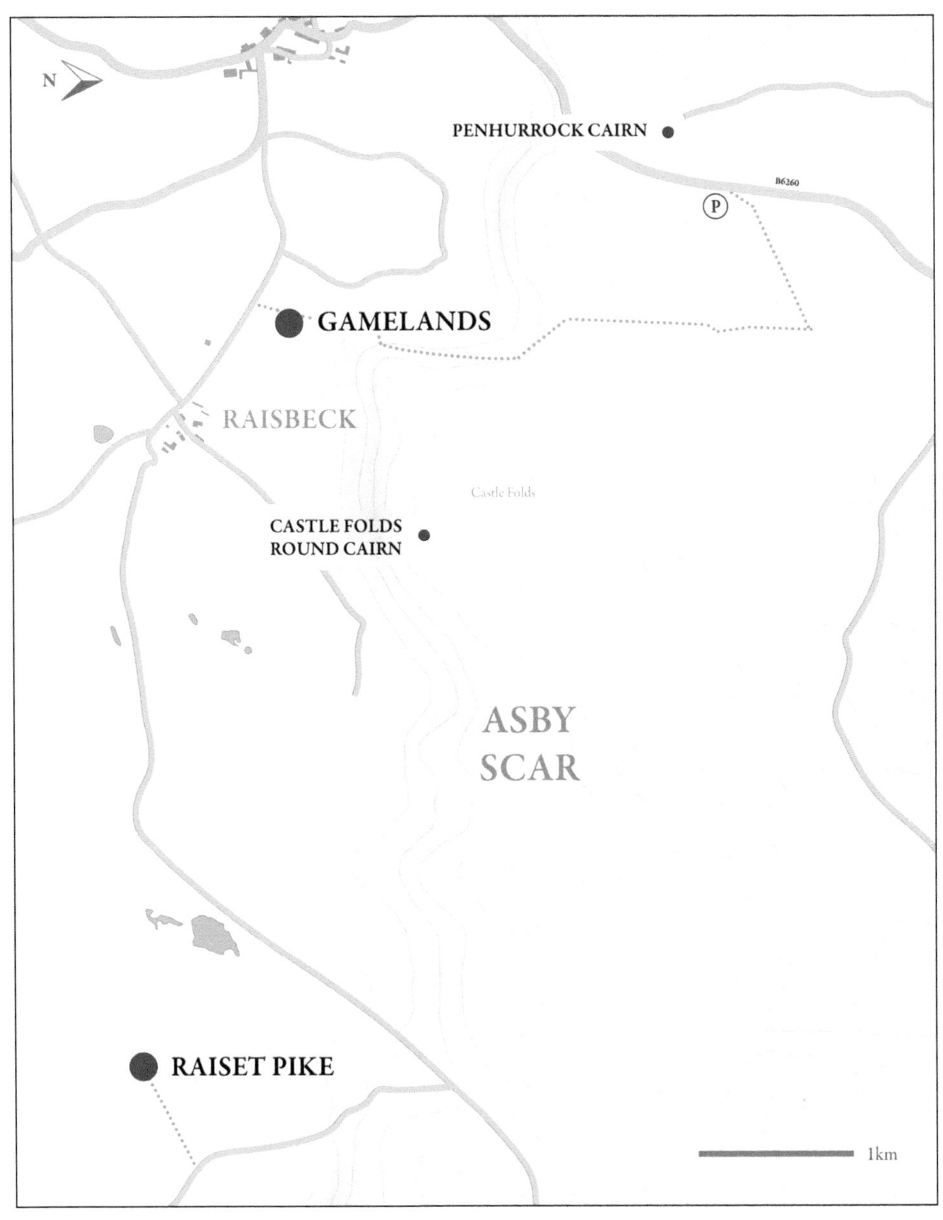
N
PENHURROCK CAIRN
B6260
P
GAMELANDS
RAISBECK
Castle Folds
CASTLE FOLDS
ROUND CAIRN
ASBY
SCAR
RAISET PIKE
1km

RAISET PIKE

Raiset Pike Long Cairn is a massive Neolithic burial cairn built on a small patch of moorland east of Asby Scar. Access to the cairn only requires a short walk from the nearest road to the east, and it can be seen for miles around, making locating it easy.

Raiset Pike Long Cairn is exceptionally large, standing 60m in diameter and approximately 4m tall, dwarfing most comparable monuments in England. It consists of two enormous stone cairns, which have been conjoined at their sides, giving Raiset Pike its cigar-like form. Sadly, numerous excavations in the nineteenth century have left it a mess.

For context, eleven small burial cairns can be found in the upland area surrounding Asby Scar. The majority of these were built by the communities that farmed the moorland during the Bronze Age. They share a similar appearance to those found in the Central Lake District, such as at Rydal and Bleaberry Haws. Raiset Pike however, with its immense size, stands apart from these lesser constructions, leading some researchers to believe that Raiset Pike was the work of a different culture during an earlier period.

– RAISET PIKE LONG CAIRN AS SEEN FROM THE WEST –

Archaeologists have debated Raiset Pike's original form for over a century, as its current appearance is only the result of constant disfigurement. An 1877 excavation discovered several post holes containing charcoal along the spine of the cairn. It was thought at the time that a row of stones had once existed along its top. However, recent excavations at other long cairns in southern England have revealed that these may have been the sockets for massive wooden posts. These were possibly destroyed by a fire, the charcoal in their post holes being the charred remains of this wooden row. Whether or not these posts were intentionally burned is unknowable, though it might be the case that their burning was the result of a cremation ritual.

Raiset Pike is believed to be a multi-layered construction, and excavations in the nineteenth century found evidence of an early construction date. The earliest stage consisted of two round cairns, the largest containing burned bones, and the smaller one containing unburned bones. Unlike smaller Bronze Age cairns, there were no urns or cists in the cairns. The burned bones in the largest cairn were those of adults, likely semi-cremated elsewhere and then moved to the site. The unburned bones in the smaller cairn were those of children. The burial of children alongside adults, a Neolithic tradition, was possibly performed in order to stay together into the afterlife.

– RAISET PIKE'S INTERIOR –

GAMELANDS

Gamelands is a massive stone circle located directly south of Asby Scar, close to the village of Orton. It can be found in a field just off the popular long-distance Coast to Coast path. Livestock often inhabit the field, and it stands on private land, but a small gate off the side of the nearby footpath allows access.

Gamelands is the second widest stone circle in Cumbria by width, extending 42m in diameter. It consists of thirty pink granite boulders laid low against the ground. While not often associated with the circles at Crosby Ravensworth, it is made in a similar style. Like those circles, Gamelands includes a stone of different rock variety. A limestone slab lies toppled at the circle's south-east edge, aligned to the winter solstice sunrise.

Similar Neolithic circles, such as Elva Plain or Castlerigg, are thought to have been enclosures that would have encircled gatherings during religious events, possibly during the winter or summer solstices. A shadow of doubt looms over this theory, however, as historical descriptions of the circle have varied, and what we see today may not represent a full picture.

– GAMELANDS DIAGRAMMED FROM ABOVE –

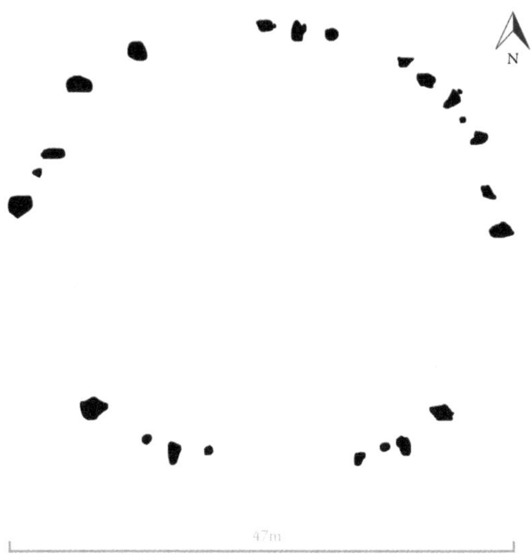

There has yet to be any modern excavation work carried out at Gamelands, though early antiquarian writings give an idea of its modern history. Several of the stones were blasted with dynamite in the nineteenth century to make way for ploughing, and the majority have fallen over in the years following.

It was noted that a massive burial cairn once stood within Gameland's interior. There has been a level of uncertainty regarding this round cairn, however, and theories on its legitimacy are especially conflicting. The earliest description of Gamelands from the owner of Orton Hall, Dr Burn, mentioned this cairn in 1777:

> *There is a tumulus … in a regular circle near 100 yards in circumference, rising gradually from the extremity to about the height of three yards in the middle. It is composed of loose stones thrown together promiscuously, and in digging lately was found one very large stone supported by one other large stone on each side, and underneath the same was a human skeleton, with the bones of several others round about.*

Burn's description may not match up with Gamelands as it stands today, but it does sound awfully similar to Raiset Pike Long Cairn. As mentioned previously, Raiset Pike is a large Neolithic burial cairn which contained the loose bones of multiple people. Could it be that the reports of the two sites had been confused by Dr Burn? Was this supposed cairn added later, during the Bronze Age? Or is Gamelands the remnants of a far more complex funerary enclosure?

Unfortunately, the true purpose of Gamelands has likely been long lost to time. R.S. Ferguson, the antiquarian who surveyed the site in 1880, stated that the locals had reconstituted the cairn stones to build their houses, noting that one of the stones from the inner cist was 'doing duty as a chimney lintel in a neighbouring house'. Gamelands was, perhaps, a victim of the modern age. Despite the eager interest of academics, the swelling tide of industrialisation carved its way, both figuratively and literally, through this circle. Despite this, Gamelands remains a fascinating circle to visit, and the easy access to Asby Scar and the views it allows are incredible.

– GAMELANDS AS VIEWED FROM ASBY SCAR –

PENHURROCK CAIRN

Found east of Asby Scar, between the B6260 and Gilts Lane, the stones that make up Penhurrock Cairn may be just the vestiges of a once wonderful monument.

While accounts will often state that this cairn is in wild disrepair, upon arrival the author was happy to find a generally orderly stone circle. While this may be the case, we certainly are not witnessing a complete monument. Much like on Iron Hill, the Penhurrock Cairn is likely just the remaining kerb of a bowl barrow. Quarrying in the nineteenth century removed the barrow, leaving only these stones.

Curiously, reports state that the kerb stones were only revealed *after* the barrow was removed. This could imply that a barrow was built over a previously existing stone circle. Indeed, Rev. James Simpson referred to Penhurrock Cairn as a stone circle, noting that it had been 'looted in the past'. Those who looted the cairn are said to have uncovered semi-burnt bones and a flat stone (which may have been either a cist or excarnation platform).

– PENHURROCK CAIRN –

OTHER SITES IN EASTERN CUMBRIA

STONE HOWE

Stone Howe is another of Shap's little-known ancient landmarks. This bizarre construction is thought to be a prehistoric burial cairn, located just up the hill from Shap's impressive abbey ruins. Historic England dates Stone Howe's creation from 4000 BC to 43 BC, emphasisng the lack of evaluation the site has received. Any chance of an archaeological investigation may be too late, however, since the cairn is all but destroyed, with only its base remaining.

SWEETHOLME STONE CIRCLE

Sweetholme Stone Circle is a challenging circle to visit for anyone who enjoys anything tangible. It was destroyed by the nearby quarry in the mid-twentieth century and would have stood directly where the quarry pit dominates the hillside. The circle was around 15m in diameter and was made up of thirty-two small pink granite stones. Seemingly, Sweetholme may have been a circle like Oddendale.

– A BIRD'S EYE VIEW OF SWEETHOLME STONE CIRCLE AS IT MAY ONCE HAVE STOOD PRIOR TO BEING SWALLOWED BY THE QUARRY –
(based on diagrams by Dr J.E. Spence)

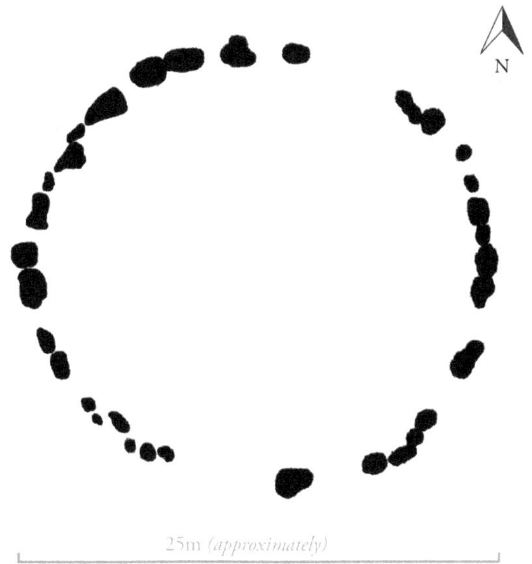

SWARTH FELL STONE CIRCLE

One of the Lake District's highest stone circles, Swarth Fell Stone Circle is a Bronze Age enclosure located next to High Street Roman Road. It requires a long and strenuous walk up Swarth Fell to access, but the views from here will make it well worth your while.

The circle itself is barely visible. Despite being made up of eighty-one stones, it will require pinpoint orienteering skills to find. It is believed that most of the circle was removed in the nineteenth century, particularly the stones on its western side. Every single stone is either leaning or fallen, which is a shame since this could have been an incredibly distinct monument. It appears to be similar to the nearby Cockpit and was likely constructed using the same unsustainable method of infilling a circular ditch.

HARDENDALE FELL STONE CIRCLE

Hardendale Fell Stone Circle was identified by Tom Clare in his 2007 book *Prehistoric Monuments of the Lake District*, although approval of these stones as a legitimate prehistoric site has yet to be confirmed. It can be found next to the junction towards Orton off the B6261.

– HARDENDALE FELL STONE CIRCLE –

HARDENDALE NAB ROUND CAIRN

Overlooking the M6 motorway, next to a tall limestone outcrop, stand four neatly constructed cairns. Underneath these prominent hill markers, you can find an Early Bronze Age round cairn. From its position at the edge of the hill, it is visible for miles around, from Moor Divock to Iron Hill. Excavations at Hardendale Nab have uncovered possible excarnation platforms, which has given researchers an important context clue into the use of similar platforms at other sites, including Oddendale, Shapbeck and Birkrigg.

CASTLE FOLDS ROUND CAIRN

A large round cairn sits just south of Castle Folds, the Roman settlement found at the peak of Asby Scar. This ruinous cairn overlooks Gamelands Stone Circle and allows for stunning views across the Pennines. An excavation in the nineteenth century discovered a cist below the cairn containing a 6ft-tall skeleton buried alongside a stone tool. Another three burials were scattered throughout the cairn.

CHAPTER 5

PENRITH

Penrith is believed to have emerged as a Roman settlement around the year AD 80. However, as evidenced by the standing stones, rock art and henges found here, the Romans were far from the original inhabitants of the region. It is evident that a large prehistoric community once resided here. The area surrounding Penrith is home to Cumbria's largest prehistoric monuments. From the henges at Eamont Bridge to the colossal stones of Long Meg, one thing is clear – this is a landscape noted for its extraordinary megalithic monuments.

Despite being grouped somewhat near to one another, visiting the megaliths around Penrith can require a fair amount of travel time. The winding country roads, one-way systems, dual carriageways and small bridges mean that any travel by car will take longer than expected. Luckily, Penrith is always close at hand, and any need for food or rest is never more than a fifteen-minute drive away.

EAMONT BRIDGE

The region between Clifton and Penrith features a vast array of prehistoric sites including the only surviving henges in Cumbria, some of northern England's heaviest standing stones and monuments that are so unique they elude mere labels.

This pastoral landscape of low, rolling fields and tall hedgerows has a similar topography to Wiltshire, home of Stonehenge and Avebury. Given such a canvas, the ancient population here chose to build sites comparable in both size and complexity to those in Wiltshire. Many of these complexes are grouped around Eamont Bridge, a small village adjacent to the River Eamont.

It is not known whether the constructions here relate to those at Shap, the Eden Valley or Moor Divock, but it is assumed that societies capable of constructing massive religious complexes like Mayburgh Henge would have had the capacity to trade and travel vast distances. Like at Langdale, Grasmere and the Furness Peninsula, elements of prehistoric Irish culture are present in the region, indicating that the sites near Eamont Bridge may represent a fusion of ancient cultures.

One thing is certain, however; the people who built the sites around Eamont Bridge were among the most impressive megalith architects in Europe.

- EAMONT BRIDGE -

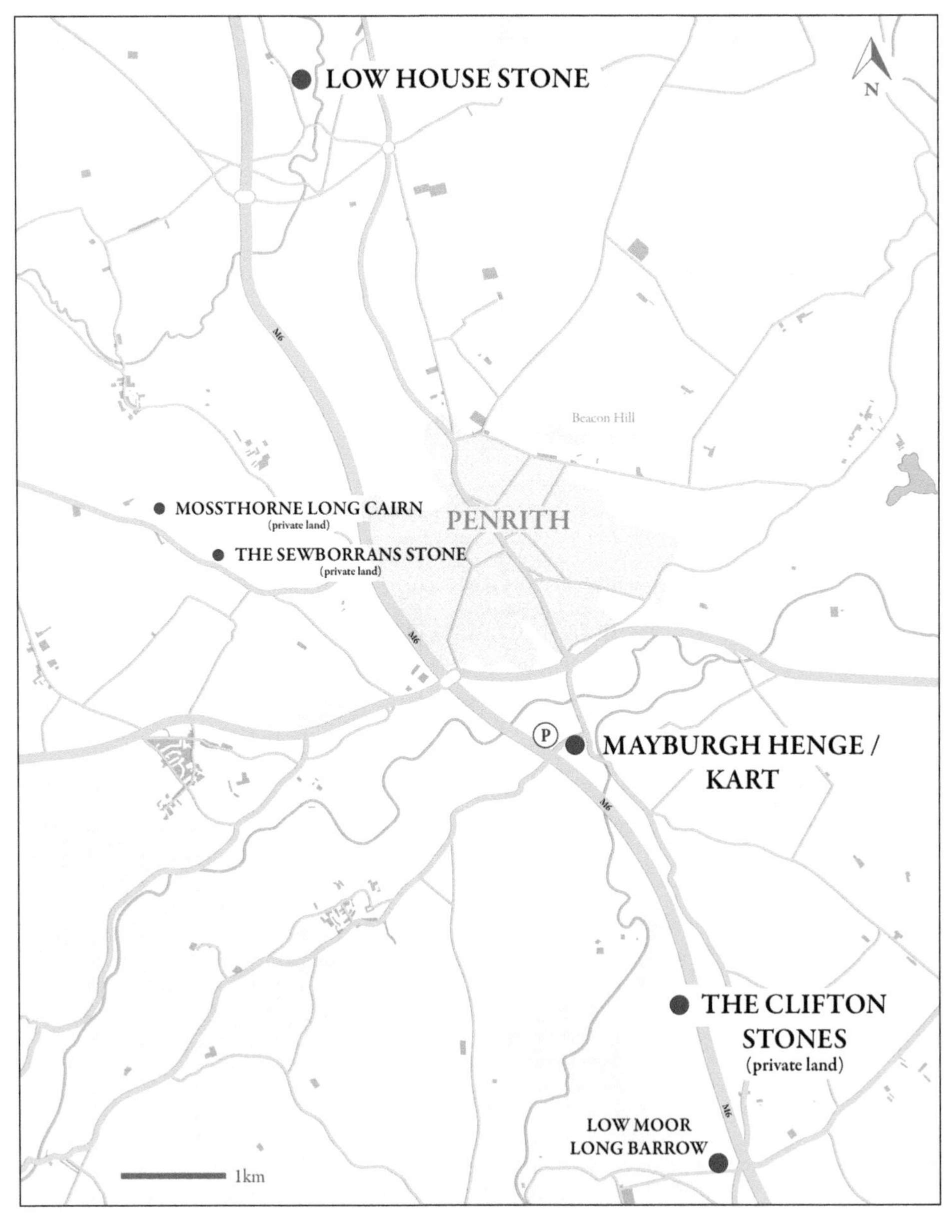

THE CLIFTON STONES

The Clifton Stones are two large sandstone megaliths located just west of the M6 motorway. They sit in a field next to the village of Clifton, between Shap and Eamont Bridge. A footpath next to the stones allows easy access from Clifton.

After years spent leaning in the damp soil, the smaller stone fell over in 1977. It is unknown if the stones had originally leaned, or if environmental factors had changed their position over time, but it was nonetheless decided to re-erect the stone in the same position and cement it into place. Thankfully, this event did result in a subsequent excavation of the area surrounding the stones. A kerb cairn was discovered directly next to the stones during the excavation. This cairn contained the partially cremated bones of several people, packed into a large cist.

It had been mentioned by antiquarians that a third stone once existed at the site, known as the hag stone. Following the re-erection of the small stone, a dig uncovered a further buried stone, which lined up towards the winter solstice.

This could be evidence that this was once part of a small stone row, the extent of which is now unknown.

These two standing stones are similar to the Giant's Grave at Kirksanton. Unlike those coastal stones, which point towards the south-west, the Clifton Stones were instead aligned to the south-east. They are also located on a low hill, allowing for a terrific view of the sun on the horizon. Their alignment towards the solstice may indicate that they were used as a simple calendar of sorts, aligning the winter solstice sunrise over the stones like the crosshairs of a rifle.

Like the entrance to Swinside or the avenue at Shap, the Clifton Stones may have served to indicate the beginning of winter, a reminder of vital importance to an agrarian society. This possibly puts the Clifton Stones into the same timeframe as those solstice-aligned monuments in the Early Bronze Age.

KING ARTHUR'S ROUND TABLE

King Arthur's Round Table (abbreviated as KART) is located at the southern end of Eamont Bridge. It is a brilliant example of a henge monument, specifically a Class II henge of the Neolithic period. Access to the site is simple: not only does KART sit within the centre of Eamont Bridge village, but the main road cuts through its northern side.

Henges are defined broadly as a ring of earth surrounding a parallel trench, creating an enclosure that resembles an island of earth. They are only known to exist in the British Isles, and though they are well known, surviving examples are relatively rare. When you begin to break henges down into subcategories, their rarity becomes even more apparent. KART is a Class II henge, a henge with two entrances opposite one another. If not for the damage caused by the Victorians, its shape would have given it the appearance of a two-door theatre in the round. This shape is roughly the same for all henges, an earthen stage of sorts, surrounded by a high embankment, though some henges have several more entranceways.

– KING ARTHUR'S ROUND TABLE –

Researchers have theorised that henge embankments may have served to block out the surrounding landscape, creating an enclosure that draws the spectator's attention towards the sky. Considering that KART's entranceways align towards the south-east, in a similar fashion to Swinside and the avenues at Moor Divock and Shap, it is possible that this enclosure was used to mark the winter solstice sunrise. If those who gathered within these enclosures were awaiting the morning sunrise, it is obvious to assume that they also witnessed the night sky, not only making this an ideal location to witness the sunrise and sunset, but also the stars.

A now lost earthwork once stood 120m to the south, known as Little Round Table, which would have undoubtedly played a role in ceremonies carried out at KART. Faint traces of this circular earthwork are still visible via satellite imagery in the form of crop marks. Illustrations of Little Round Table from the eighteenth century show just a simple circle without an embankment. To what extent this is accurate is not known, as an embankment could easily have been removed to make way for ploughing.

The two Round Table earthworks are part of the Eamont Bridge Ritual Landscape along with the nearby Mayburgh Henge, which sits less than 400m to the west. Before the village was expanded it was known to be within sight of Mayburgh Henge, the entrance of which leads directly west towards KART.

Author's Notes: When looking onto the field from the road, it is not immediately obvious that you are witnessing a wonder of British archaeology, and it appears to be nothing more than a grazing field. I recommend that you head to its southern end, where on the raised edges of the entrance you can get a better picture of how the site would have looked. I also advise visiting at either sunrise or sunset, as the low sun casts shadows, making the trenches more visible.

MAYBURGH HENGE

Simply put, Mayburgh Henge is one of the most awe-inspiring prehistoric monuments in Britain. Easily accessed and not typically busy, you will often be able to admire this stunning site all by yourself (albeit in the company of cows). Despite being incongruously located next to the M6 motorway, Mayburgh has not lost any of its breathtaking aura; its massive banks serve to separate you from your surroundings and make you feel completely distant from the modern world.

This stone enclosure is more like a megalithic stadium than a henge, with banks as high as a two-storey house and an area greater than three football pitches (approximately 120m in diameter on all axes). It was constructed using over 20,000 tonnes of stone that had to be hauled by hand over 300m from the nearby River Lowther, a task that would require an incredibly large work-force to accomplish.

Mayburgh is not a henge by any classical definition of the word. It is, in fact, a common misnomer to describe Mayburgh as the heaviest henge in Britain.

Henge monuments are typically made with soil and other earthen materials. Mayburgh Henge, on the other hand, is made entirely of stone. It also has no inner bank, no inner platform, and only a single entrance, further demonstrating that this is not a henge. Perhaps the most apt label for Mayburgh is an Irish-style henge.

Unlike their English counterparts, Irish henges do not contain inner trenches. Like Mayburgh, these massive rings sit on flat ground, forming a large enclosure. Unlike Mayburgh, they are typically made of earth, but their design and purpose are unquestionably comparable. This is a fascinating link, which may be more than a coincidence, as other Irish-inspired rock art motifs can be found in Cumbria, such as at Copt Howe, Grasmere, Little Meg and Glassonby. Dowth Henge, which can be found next to the famous Newgrange, is perhaps the most comparable enclosure in the British Isles.

Mayburgh Henge does not align with the solstice sun, unlike many similar monuments. Instead, the entrance points westwards, towards KART. This suggests that these two monuments have been designed to be used in conjunction with each other. KART, a true Neolithic henge, is aligned with the sunrise of the winter solstice, indicating that both sites may have been used together during solstice celebrations.

Despite being well preserved, the more you study the history of Mayburgh, the sadder the story becomes. The outer bank, for example, has been clearly gnarled over the centuries, probably because of the removal of trees from the embankment. This has dragged tonnes of rock out of the enclosure, leaving large holes along its spine. The site was also plagued by looting during the eighteenth century, as people dug into the embankment in the hope of finding ancient treasures.

A lone megalith stands at the centre of the enclosure, a feature of much discussion. In 1725 William Stukeley, famous for his work on Avebury, described two stone circles within Mayburgh, each consisting of four exceptionally large megaliths. This suggests that the remaining stone is the only survivor of an original eight, which would have once formed two circles. A Welsh explorer named Thomas Pennant elaborated on Stukeley's survey, noting in his 1796 *Tour of Scotland* that one of these stone circles had an adjacent avenue, which continued out from Mayburgh's entrance. This avenue would have led towards KART.

Mayburgh Henge may have been constructed to host ceremonies involving hundreds of people. It is perhaps best to compare Mayburgh to similar ceremonial enclosures in Cumbria, such as Shap Avenue or Swinside. If Mayburgh was used in a comparable way, we can assume that people would have followed a path through the Eamont Bridge Ritual Landscape during the sunrise on the winter solstice. It is likely, then, that Mayburgh Henge and KART were designed to accommodate a wide processional path, which would have either started or ended at Mayburgh Henge. People may have walked between the two enclosures, witnessing the sun rising to the south-east over the horizon. Not unlike Kemp Howe Stone Circle, which functioned as the terminal to Shap Avenue, Mayburgh Henge may have also served to cap off this processional path from KART.

– MAYBURGH HENGE'S REMAINING STANDING STONE –

LOW MOOR

An enormous mound of earth thought by some to be a Neolithic burial monument, Low Moor, also known as Trainford Brow, sits parallel to the road towards Askham village, west of the A6.

Some believe that Low Moor is a massive example of a long barrow, while others insist that it is not a prehistoric monument at all. Long barrows usually date to the Neolithic, and are among the rarest burial monuments in Britain, making them especially important in our understanding of the period. They typically contain chambers, which hold the bodies of many people. No proof of this has been found at Low Moor, although excavations have never been carried out.

It is 100m in length and 25m across, technically making it one of the largest prehistoric burial monuments in Britain. It points towards the east, similar to the more famous West Kennet Long Barrow in Wiltshire, and the nearby Mayburgh Henge.

– LOW MOOR LONG BARROW –

When compared to other long barrows in Cumbria, Low Moor is clearly an anomaly. Not only is it massive and extremely well defined, but also seemingly undisturbed. Perhaps because of this, serious doubt has arisen as to whether Low Moor is a legitimate prehistoric monument at all. Many argue that it is nothing more than a spoil dump from the time the adjacent road was built … *but with what evidence?* The volume of the earthen mound seems to correlate to the width of the nearby road, and after all, how could a monument so rare, and so massive, go unrecognised for so long?

Despite being controversially labelled as a long barrow, it *is* scheduled, and as such is protected as a historic site by law. If Low Moor is a genuine prehistoric monument, it could represent one of Britain's oldest burial traditions, possibly dating back to as early as 3400 BC. If it is the result of road development, then it is a fine coincidence that it looks exactly like an ancient long barrow. All the characteristic features of long barrows can be seen here: a long mound with flanking trenches, a sloping angle, and a flat front. Unfortunately, only modern excavations may reveal the truth.

Author's Notes: The barrow is almost entirely covered by trees and brambles, which make it imperceptible during the summer months. That is not to suggest that its apparency is much better during the winter, as there are still over fifty trees growing from its top. It is quite possible that Low Moor Long Barrow has been hidden in plain sight since the Neolithic period.

LOWHOUSE STONE

The Lowhouse Stone is an 8ft tall granite menhir located underneath a large oak tree, north of Penrith. It is one of the largest megaliths in Cumbria, making it easy to spot from the nearby road. Alternatively, when travelling by train between Carlisle and Penrith, you can catch a fleeting glimpse of the stone from the carriage window.

The function of the Lowhouse Stone is not well understood. There have been no excavations in the surrounding area, so the existence of other post holes or stones is not out of the question. Some have speculated that it was a boundary stone, a barrier between land or county lines, typically dating between the medieval and Victorian periods. That is, of course, a ludicrous idea. It is an absurd illusion to suggest that this immense granite megalith was erected merely to demarcate boundaries. More likely is the idea that the Lowhouse Stone is an example of a Neolithic menhir, a lone standing stone. The purpose of these lonely stones is not known, but they probably served a variety of religious purposes among prehistoric communities.

- THE LOWHOUSE STONE -

A collection of packing stones jut up from the base of the Lowhouse Stone, which is a dead give-away that it was erected by prehistoric hands. Packing stones were used to hold the stone in place and are present at the base of most megaliths across Britain. If you ever suspect a rock is a prehistoric standing stone, then this is the first thing you should check for, as the majority of prehistoric menhirs were held in place using packing stones. Standing stones like this were erected across Europe from the Early Neolithic all the way up to the Bronze Age. This unfortunately means that dating the Lowhouse Stone is almost impossible without a modern excavation.

Author's Notes: The Lowhouse Stone is a relatively good litmus test of how interested a person is in the study of old stones. To those intrigued by prehistory, this massive standing stone, positioned so close to modern developments, has remained steadfast in its ability to capture the essence of a landscape sculpted by people long forgotten. From such humble beginnings, western civilisation was able to blossom; time ceases for no one stone, but through the study of these megaliths we can understand how far we have come in such a short period.

THE SEWBORRANS STONE

The stone at Sewborrans is yet another remote megalith found to the north of Eamont Bridge. It is an excellent example of the fascinating megalithic tradition of lone standing stones being erected, their size demonstrating just how impressive this feat of lifting was. However, like the Lowhouse Stone, there is little context to help us understand its purpose.

Several nearby stones lie to the immediate east, which have been speculatively linked to the Sewborrans Stone. Piled into a small cairn near the adjacent fence, some suggest they were placed here during the designation of the field boundaries. As this field was designated at some point during the nineteenth century, we can assume that they were only recently moved to their current position. It is possible that the stones are the remnants of a larger monument, perhaps a stone circle or avenue.

MOSSTHORNE LONG CAIRNS

The Mossthorne Long Cairns are located directly north-east of the Sewborrans Stone. The cairns are on private land, but you can easily see the largest from the nearby road. The smaller cairn is not visible without venturing into private fields, so ask for permission if you would like to get close.

Unlike long barrows, such as Low Moor, long cairns were mostly created using loose stones and often have a slug-like shape. The Mossthorne Long Cairns are no different, their uneven shape suggesting that they may have be constructed over several stages, in a similar style to Raiset Pike near Asby Scar.

There were reports that urns and Langdale axe heads were discovered here in the nineteenth century, suggesting that this area was inhabited during the transition between the Neolithic, when stone axes were popular burial accessories, and the Bronze Age, when decorated urns were common in burials. This could imply that these cairns belong to the Early Bronze Age, a period that likely saw the construction of the nearby Mayburgh Henge and Long Meg.

– MOSSTHORNE SOUTH LONG CAIRN –

BROOMRIGG PLANTATION

Broomrigg Plantation is a small area of forestry located between Penrith and Carlisle. Four stone circles survive amongst the forests, listed from Broomrigg A to Broomrigg D. While mostly ruinous, excavations on the stone circles here have helped researchers understand their purpose.

While we will only be focusing on the key prehistoric monuments at Broomrigg, there are several more standing stones, burial mounds and kerb cairns scattered throughout the forest. Several hut circles, like those found on Bleaberry Haws, were built to the south of the plantation, the circular remains of round houses.

A landscape strikingly similar to Lacra Bank, Burnmoor, Crosby Ravensworth, and Moor Divock, Broomrigg Plantation was probably an Early Bronze Age complex used to process the dead. You may wonder why, exactly, there are so many of these funerary complexes found throughout Cumbria. In the modern day we expect there to be facilities available in the event of a death, those being: crematoriums, churches, coffin workshops and graveyards. This was, naturally, the same during prehistory, as the need to deal with the dead has always been an issue requiring tremendous time and energy.

Considering the number of cremations taking place within these sites, it is likely that only the most eminent members of a tribe would have access to such facilities. But nevertheless, every community seemed to have its own funerary centre at hand.

– BROOMRIGG PLANTATION –

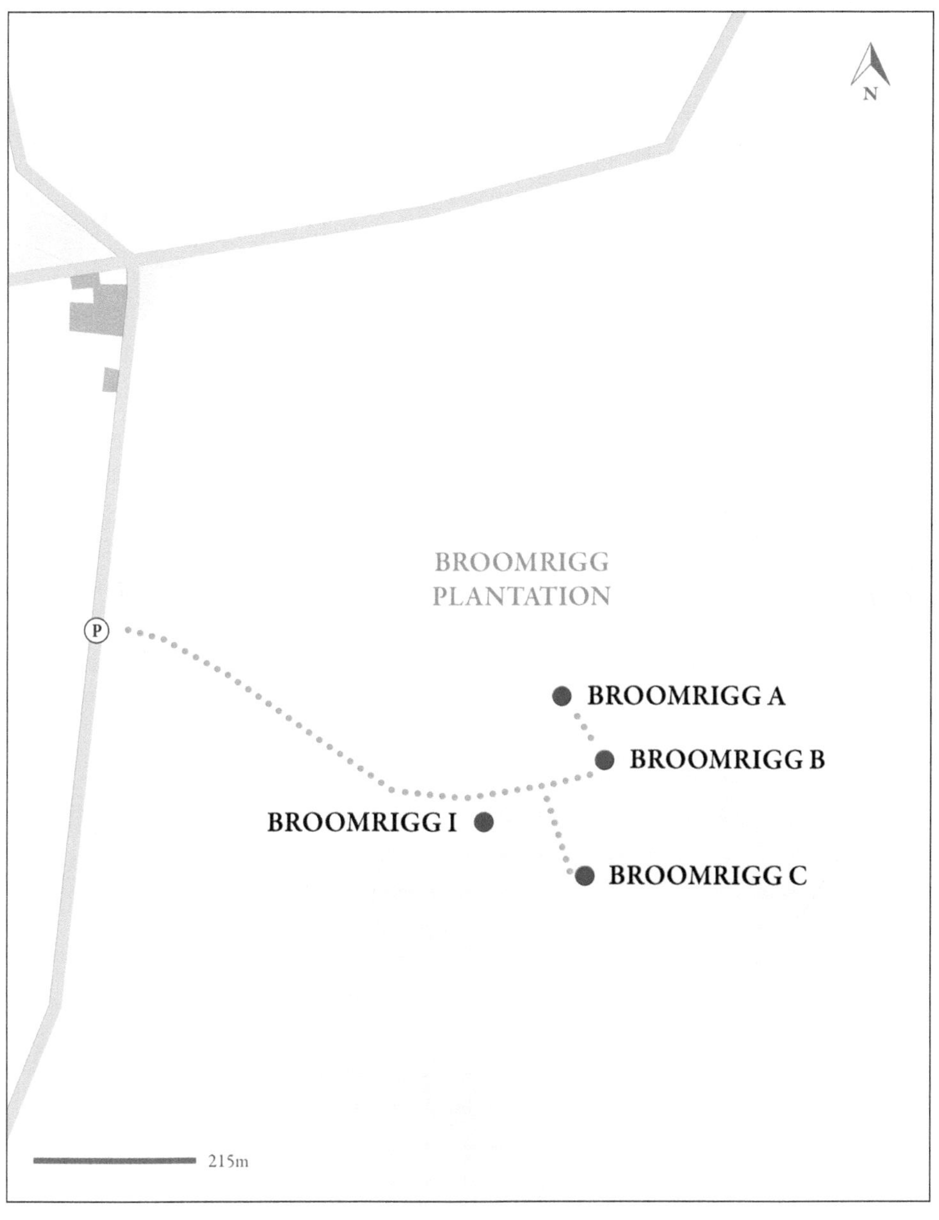

BROOMRIGG B

Adjacent to a collapsed wall just off the main path through Broomrigg Plantation, you can find a stone circle known as Broomrigg B. It is the easiest monument to find at Broomrigg Plantation, requiring only several steps off the main path to access.

Broomrigg B is just the remains of a damaged burial monument, with only a few large sandstone megaliths surviving. Four stones, of an original seven, are roughly arranged into a circle. They are thought to be kerb stones, which would have once held a cairn or mound in place. The sandstone megalith's pink hue is eye-catching, contrasting heavily against the surrounding greenery. Comparable monuments, such as the bowl barrows on Iron Hill, date to the Early Bronze Age.

Broomrigg B was excavated in 1952 by archaeologist K.S. Hodgson. Perhaps the most fascinating find of the excavation was a small stone, exhibiting several X-shaped carvings. Unlike the large decorated stones found across northern

England, this may have been what is known as portable art, a carved stone small enough to carry by hand. If the stone had been used as a pendant, you would expect holes to be present, capable of threading string, but no such holes were found on this stone.

If this is authentic prehistoric rock art, it begs the simple question: *why was it buried here?* Perhaps these carvings may have been the work of a single artist rock doodling in their spare time, and the inspired individual who created this artwork was possibly buried within Broomrigg B. Unfortunately, like most personal stories left untold, such questions will most likely remain unanswered.

THE CARVED MOTIFS

BROOMRIGG C

Broomrigg C is the best preserved and perhaps most noteworthy of the Broomrigg Plantation stone circles. Hidden deep within the forest to the south of the main path, it sits within a dense patch of woodland bracken, making it virtually invisible from July to October.

Fourteen stones are arranged into a circular configuration surrounding a raised area of land. Judging by the densely grouped curve of stones along the south-east edge of the circle, Broomrigg C was once comprised of many tightly arranged stones, although most are now missing or buried. A 1948 excavation unearthed several small urns from within Broomrigg C, as well as bone fragments and nuggets of bronze around its inner area. One of these urns was decorated with a herringbone motif, where several intersecting triangles converge in a row. Pottery of this style was popular during the Middle Bronze Age.

Nestled in the south-western quadrant of the circle is a cairn surrounded by a ring of kerb stones. Like the burials found within Brat's Hill (on Burnmoor), this was probably a kerb cairn. Inside this cairn was found a layer of sand. Curiously, other burial circles, such as Grey Croft and Askham Fell Ring Cairn were also found to contain a layer of sand. At both sites there was evidence of intense burning on top of this sand layer, indicating that these monuments were used as cremation pyres.

This cairn was added during an earlier phase of Broomrigg C, as the circle we see today was built over the top of the cairn's kerb stones. Nobody knows why a larger stone circle was constructed over these earlier phases, and excavations have only raised more questions than answers. The circle we see today could have been added hundreds of years after the inner burial cairns were constructed.

– BROOMRIGG C DIAGRAMMED FROM ABOVE –

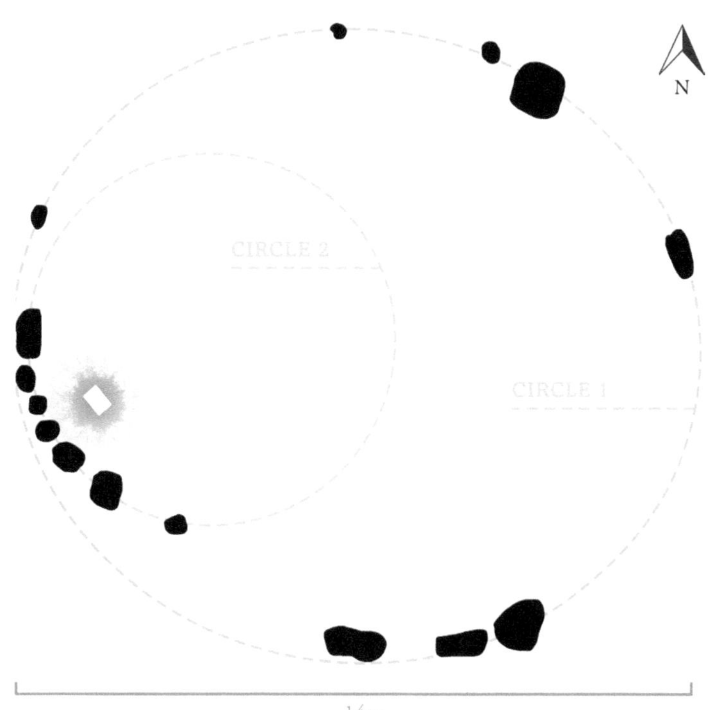

BROOMRIGG A

Broomrigg A is located at the centre of the plantation. It is the largest of the circles at Broomrigg Plantation, but by far the least remarkable. A short walk over extremely uneven terrain will be required to access the circle, which is not worth the risk to access, especially considering the circle's dilapidated state. Unfortunately, only four of the stones remain in situ above the ground, all of which now lie recumbent.

A long time ago, Broomrigg A was possibly an impressive circle, standing 55m in diameter with a stone row trailing off towards the north-west. Its size technically makes Broomrigg A the second-widest stone circle in Cumbria (over Gamelands), although its current state leaves it almost unrecognisable. To the west is a smaller kerb cairn; again, like the circle, it is ruinous and difficult to spot in the foliage.

Broomrigg C is a better-preserved example of what Broomrigg A once was: a low-lying stone circle that likely saw multiple uses throughout the Early Bronze Age; an area used for cremations and burials. For a better idea of Broomrigg A's function, studying Brat's Hill or Studfold would make for a clearer assessment.

–BROOMRIGG AS DIAGRAMMED FROM ABOVE –

BROOMRIGG I

Broomrigg I is a lone megalith located in the woods immediately north of Broomrigg C. Forestry laws (as of 2020) require surveyors to mark any possible historical remains with red posts in order to avoid damage, so its location should be clearly marked.

This stone once stood over 6ft tall, making it the tallest megalith at Broomrigg plantation. Lone standing stones are rare in Cumbria, and here we can assume it was once a component of either a stone row, a cairn or a lost stone circle. Interestingly, a large area of land has been marked with red posts to the north of the stone, hinting at a possible stone row discovery. There has been no word on this as of 2020, but considering Broomrigg's overgrown state, there is possibly far more left to uncover in this forest.

– BROOMRIGG I AND ONE OF THE MANY RED POSTS –

EDEN VALLEY

The Eden Valley follows Cumbria's longest river, the River Eden, stretching 145km south to north, winding through almost all of Cumbria's length. The portion we will be focusing on is found just north of Penrith.

An area of rolling hills dominated by large waterways, the Eden Valley certainly has a congenial atmosphere. Not unlike Eamont Bridge, the Eden Valley shares a topographic resemblance to Wiltshire, home of Stonehenge. Regions this fertile, open and level were not only popular areas to settle, but those who lived here saw great potential for building.

And build they did. Here, among the winding waterways and thickets of woodland, you can find some of Britain's most immense megalithic monuments. While areas such as Bleaberry Haws, in the Central Lakes, are known for their miniaturised monuments, those found here may be considered maximised.

Carvings appear on every site in the region, almost all of which are complex. As at Furness, Grasmere, Langdale and Eamont Bridge, the carvings in the Eden Valley may have been influenced by Irish settlers or traders during the Neolithic period. However, unlike the somewhat subtle influences seen elsewhere, they are among the most distinct features put on display here.

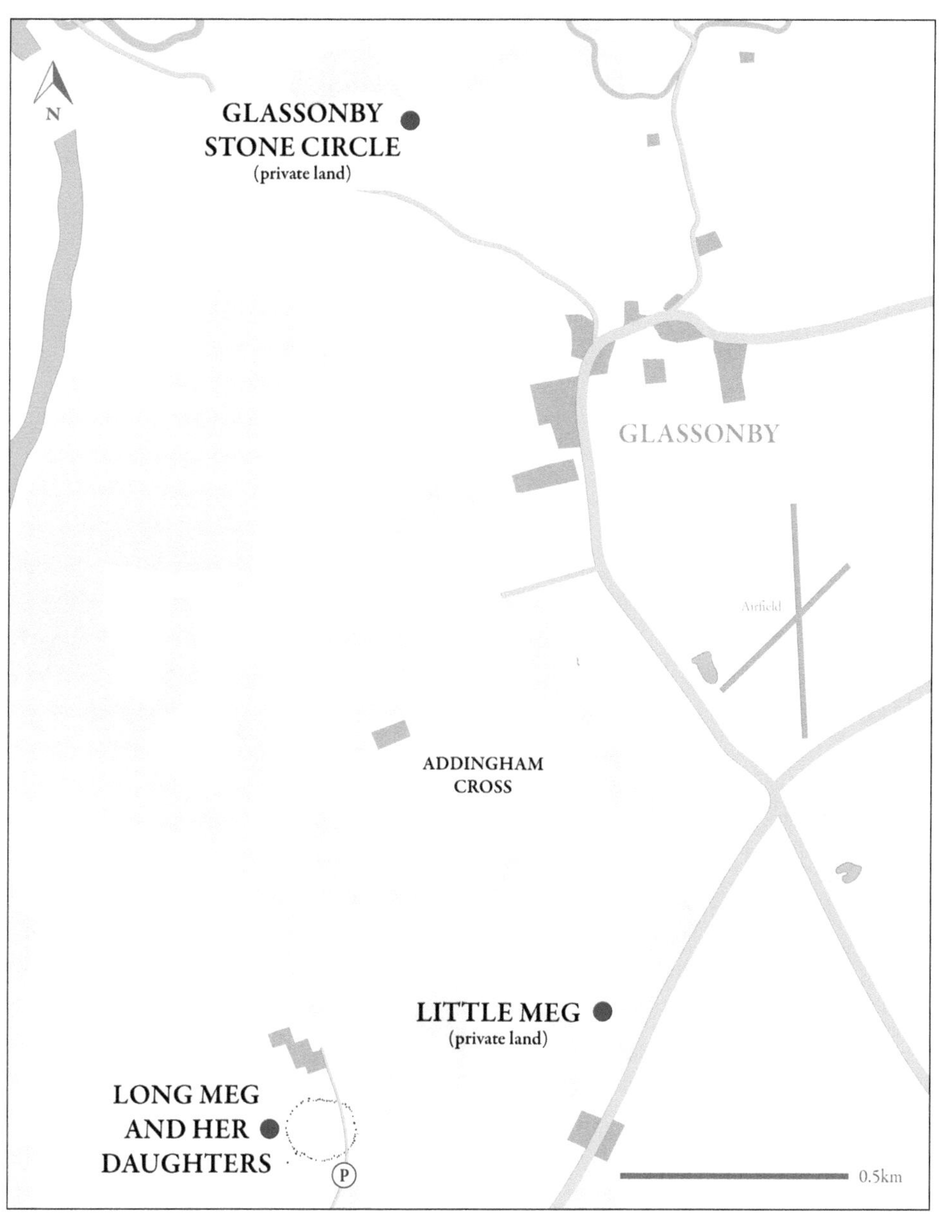
N
GLASSONBY
STONE CIRCLE
(private land)
GLASSONBY
Airfield
ADDINGHAM
CROSS
LITTLE MEG
(private land)
LONG MEG
AND HER
DAUGHTERS
P
0.5km

LONG MEG AND HER DAUGHTERS

Long Meg and Her Daughters (usually shortened to just Long Meg) is the largest stone circle in Cumbria. Only two larger stone circles survive in England: Avebury in Wiltshire and Stanton Drew in Somerset. When compared to those better-known sites, however, Long Meg stands out as being particularly well preserved.

The monument's peculiar name refers to its two most distinct features: a tall megalith known as Long Meg, and an adjacent stone circle known as the Daughters. The stone circle consists of an incredible sixty-six megaliths, which is especially impressive when you consider that most large stone circles retain less than 50 per cent of their original stones. Moreover, these are megaliths in the truest sense, with even the smallest of the stones dwarfing those in the majority of stone circles across Britain.

An unmistakable entrance is found at Long Meg's south-western edge, created by placing two stones outside the circle, as if forming an avenue outward. It is remarkably similar in style to the entrance found at Swinside near Millom. Like Swinside, Long Meg's entrance points to the winter solstice sun, although in this case Long Meg is aligned towards the sunset, not the sunrise.

– LONG MEG AND HER DAUGHTERS DIAGRAMMED FROM ABOVE–

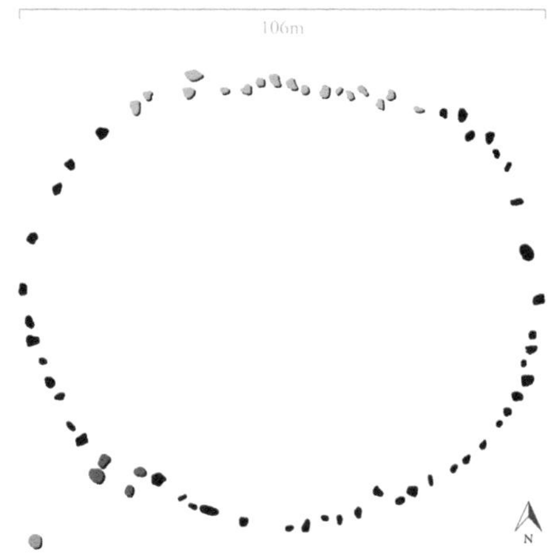

GREEN: FALLEN NORTHERN STONES
RED: ENTRANCE WAY 'PORTAL STONES'
BLUE: LONG MEG MENHIR

Despite the age of the circle remaining unknown, it is often inaccurately dated to the Middle Bronze Age (around 1500 BC). The truth is no doubt far more complicated, and it could be argued that Long Meg is among Britain's oldest stone circles. Surveys have indicated that the stone circle was once set within a Neolithic henge monument, making up an inner ring of stones running parallel to the banks of the henge. These trace elements of a lost henge are just one component of an astonishing complex of prehistoric earthworks thought to date as far back as the Early Neolithic period. Long Meg is far from a lone monument.

Firstly, there remains evidence of a massive circular earthwork immediately north of the circle. This earthwork was over 220m in diameter and may have been what is colloquially known as a super-henge. Evidence for this can be seen today in the pattern of fallen stones along the perimeter of the circle, and a second entrance at the north-west edge of the circle that aligns with a gap in the enclosure. While many of the stones remain standing, those on the north side have all toppled. This is thought to be the result of the stones falling into the area where the super-henge had once been; every stone falling outwards towards the enclosure's ditch.

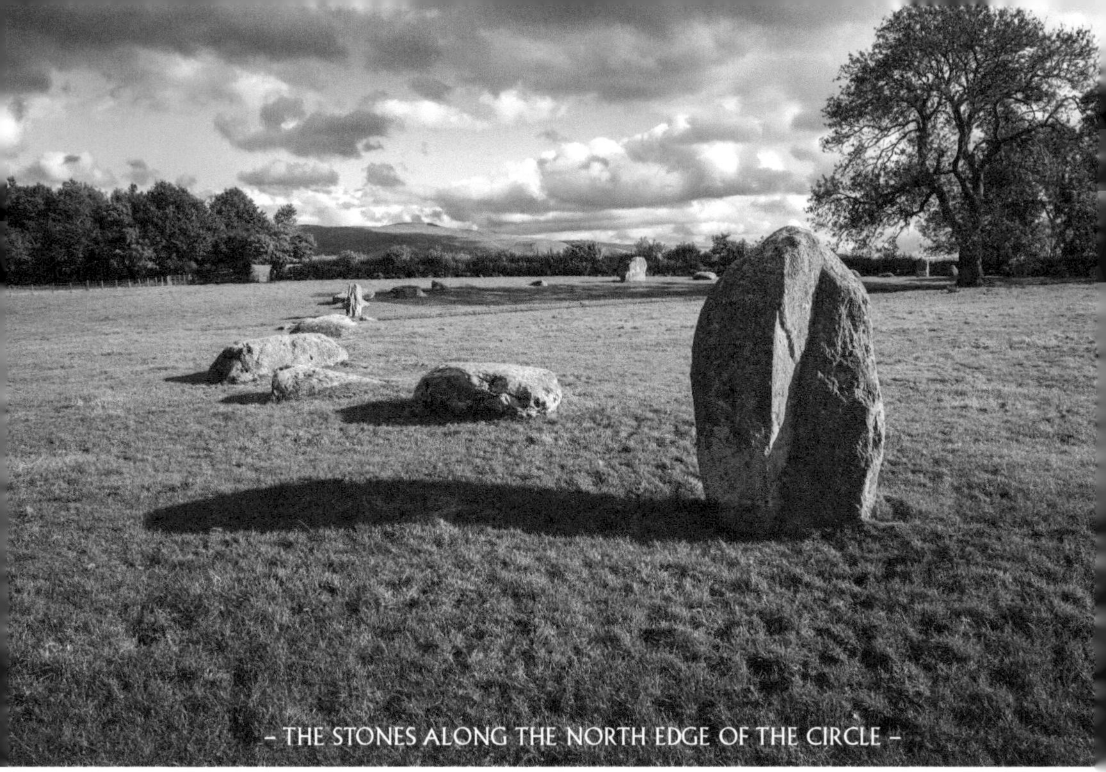

– THE STONES ALONG THE NORTH EDGE OF THE CIRCLE –

Secondly, like Stonehenge, Long Meg may have had an adjacent cursus monument. A cursus is an earthwork made by digging elongated trenches, forming a cigar-shaped arena in the earth. They are among the least understood monuments ancient Britain has to offer. Cursus monuments tend to date to the

– THE ENCLOSURES –

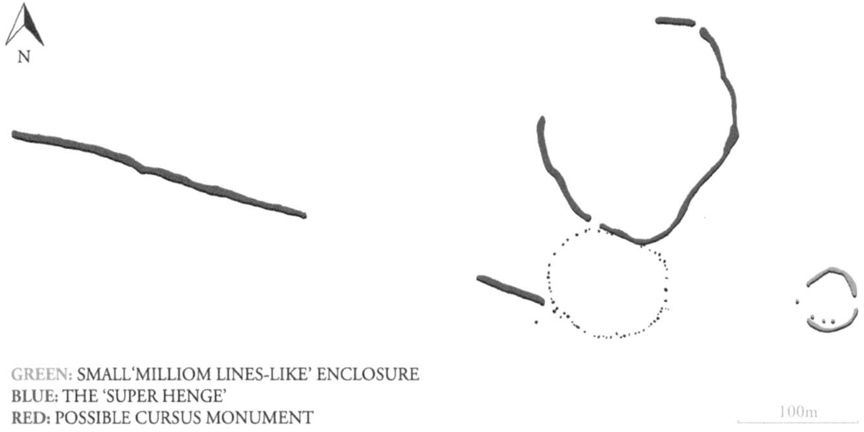

Neolithic period, and are thought to only exist in areas of immense importance to the ancient Britons. Later stone avenues may have replaced these more primitive earthworks during the Early Bronze age. Some have argued that the cursus at Long Meg is, in fact, nothing more than the remains of a pipeline excavation. No conclusive proof has confirmed either possibility.

These two earthworks that sandwich the stone circle are ostensibly older. The north side of the stone circle is squashed as if trying to avoid overlapping with the super-henge, seemingly having been designed after the earthworks had been created. Again, like Stonehenge, the addition of a stone circle may have been a renovation of sorts. A timber circle / henge monument (not unlike the Millom Lines) may have been replaced with stones during the Early Bronze Age.

A 2016 excavation radiocarbon dated the earliest known presence at the site to around 5200 BC. While the stone circle was undoubtably built later, people had clearly inhabited this site since the Mesolithic period. Evidence of monument construction was dated to 3950 BC to 3790 BC – a range of time when the nearby earthworks were likely created. There was not, however, any conclusive way to date the stones.

Immediately south-west of the entrance stands the eponymous Long Meg, a 12ft tall standing stone. She is Cumbria's tallest megalith. Yet even still, some believe that she is buried as deep as she stands, implying that Long Meg may be over 20ft tall!

– CARVED MOTIF ON LONG MEG –

The stone is adorned with a complex array of ring-mark carvings. These rings are not accompanied by the typical display of cup marks that come paired with ring markings. Instead, much like at Copt Howe, the visible carvings on Long Meg appear as concentric rings. The carvings we see on Long Meg today, however, only make up a small portion of the art, which are the less weathered and probably more recent carvings. Using 3D scanning technology, researchers have been able to get a better picture of the carvings, revealing several spiral motifs.

Author's Notes: Solstice sunsets cast long shadows. This is something that ancient people would certainly have noticed, and a fact that some believe to be a crucial element in understanding Long Meg's purpose. During the sunset solstice, Long Meg's shadow would have stretched between the entrance's portal stones, towards the centre of the circle. Like the sights on a rifle, you can stand at the centre of the circle and witness the sun casting a shadow straight to your feet, a perfect marker for when the solstice arrives – and thus a simple but effective calendar. If we are to believe that celebrations took place here on a mass scale, as the circle's size suggests, then it is probable that such a perfect union of heaven and earth would have provided worshippers with a sense of religious fulfilment.

GLASSONBY STONE CIRCLE

Glassonby Stone Circle is located approximately 2km north of Long Meg. No public footpaths allow good visibility of the monument, but you can just about see it over the wall from the road to the south.

The stones of this "stone circle" are the partial remains of a massive Neolithic barrow, which was damaged by antiquarian G. Cheesebrough during an excavation in 1900, leaving only the kerb stones that once held the top of the mound in place. Despite being at the cost of the monument, Cheesbrough's dig unearthed many curious artifacts from the site.

Two cremated remains were unearthed just outside the circle. One was placed into a large urn, while the other was simply buried in a rock-cut pit. Within the centre of the circle an empty cist was found, having been the victim of grave robbing. An ornate jewellery bead, found within an area of burning, was also discovered; possibly an area used for cremations. Perhaps the most interesting find, however, was a set of rock carvings, shallowly etched onto one of the kerb stones.

The carvings are unlike anything else found in Cumbria: semi-ovoid motifs stacked one on top of another, giving them the illusion of depth. Still, as with rock carvings found in the Lake District, such as Copt Howe, these motifs are like those found within Neolithic burial chambers. Below the ovoid carvings is an inverted triangle, next to which are several chevron carvings, parallel stacks of V shaped lines.

Again, carvings like these are not seen elsewhere in Cumbria and are more often associated with Neolithic tombs in Ireland. Not only are the carvings seemingly Irish in origin, but the circle is also in a style more commonly seen in Ireland. Considering the lack of comparable monuments in northern England, one

– GLASSONBY CARVINGS –

could suggest that Glassonby was the product of Irish settlers or traders sometime in the Neolithic period.

LITTLE MEG

Little Meg is a small stone circle found north-east of Long Meg, lying in a private field just off the road between Glassonby and Little Salkeld.

Not a stone circle in the classic sense, Little Meg is instead the remains of a burial mound (much like Glassonby). The mound that once stood between the stones was removed by antiquarians during the nineteenth century, who left the stones out of

– LITTLE MEG –

place. Little Meg's original purpose was to simply retain this lost mound. Thankfully, the removal of the mound was not completely in vain. In doing so, antiquarians uncovered two ornately decorated capstones, which covered a cist. An urn, decorated in a style typical of the Early Bronze Age, was found interred within this cist.

– THE CARVING ON LITTLE MEG –

One of the eleven remaining stones of Little Meg features a double spiral carving. This is easily the most distinct piece of rock art in Cumbria, being near perfectly recognisable, no matter the weather conditions.

Spiral carvings are only found at a few prehistoric sites in England, appearing far more commonly within large Neolithic tombs. Perhaps the best-known examples are the spirals that adorn the walls of Newgrange, a monumental passage tomb in Ireland. Once again, much like Glassonby, Mayburgh Henge, Grasmere and Copt Howe, the carvings on Little Meg are possibly of Irish origins.

Many regions in Cumbria were potentially influenced by Irish migrants during prehistory. This would help explain the lack of distinctly English rock art in the county, and the prevalence of art associated with Neolithic Irish tombs. Undoubtedly, influences like these did not only occur through isolated incidents. Constant trade between Britain and Ireland likely caused a fusion of prehistoric cultures over time, especially along Britain's west coast. If this was the case, we can assume that Castlerigg, Swinside, Shap Avenue, The Millom Lines, and Burnmoor, etc. were all, to some degree, a result of this fusion (although the jury is certainly still out on this theory.)

– THE CARVING ON THE EDENHALL STONE, UNEARTHED IN 1909 –

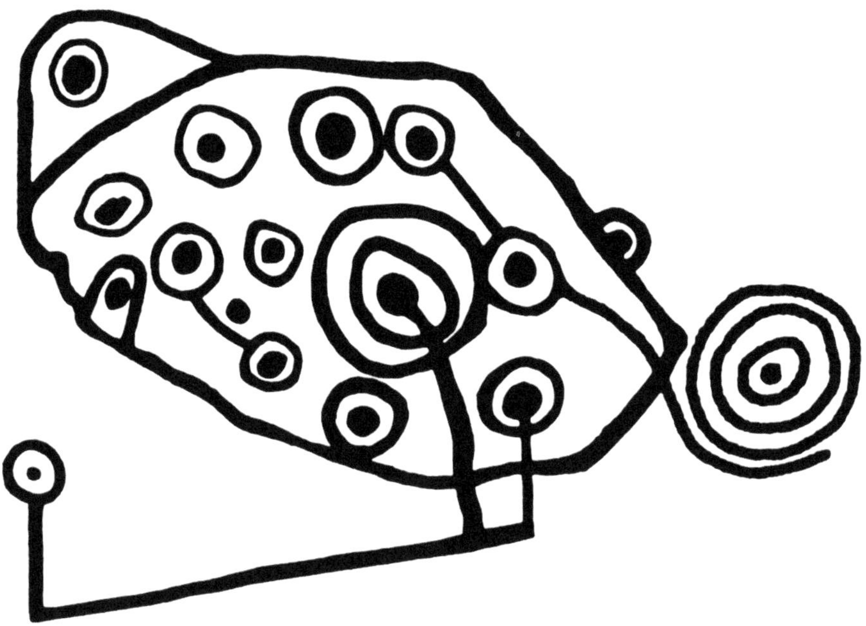

Author's Notes: Further examples of intricate carvings in the area include the Kirkoswald and Edenhall stones. Now on display at Tullie House Museum in Carlisle, they were each discovered under cairns within 4 miles of Little Meg. Again, these motifs are uncommonly complex, exhibiting patterns rare in the region, perhaps a fusion of English and Irish motifs.

OTHER SITES NEAR PENRITH

LEACET HILL STONE CIRCLE

You can find this small circle of kerb stones in the plantation just south of Whinfell Forest, typically obscured by bracken, and found on private land.

Only half of the monument survives, as it was cut in two by a field boundary at some point in the nineteenth century. Excavations unearthed multiple urns, buried adjacent to four of the five stones. In total, ten urns were discovered in this small circle alone! At the centre of the circle, the remains of a cremation pyre were discovered. A solid amount of evidence indicates Leacet Hill was used for cremation ceremonies and so similar monuments are often compared to this better-understood example.

THE TORTIE STONE

A recently discovered cup and ring-marked stone 2km south of Hallbankgate village, the Tortie Stone is the most eastern example of rock art in Cumbria and is not indicative of the styles of art regularly found in the county. Unlike the Irish-inspired motifs iconic to Cumbria, the art on the Tortie Stone is in a style more commonly associated with eastern England. As it sits so close to the border with County Durham, this is not too unexpected.

GREEN HOWE BARROW

The Green Howe Barrow is a flat-topped bowl barrow found to the north of Aughtree Fell. It is situated adjacent to what is known as the Green Howe Enclosure, a defended farmstead dating back to the Roman period. The buildings here no longer exist, though you can clearly see the defensive trenches and irrigation systems sculpted into the surrounding moor.

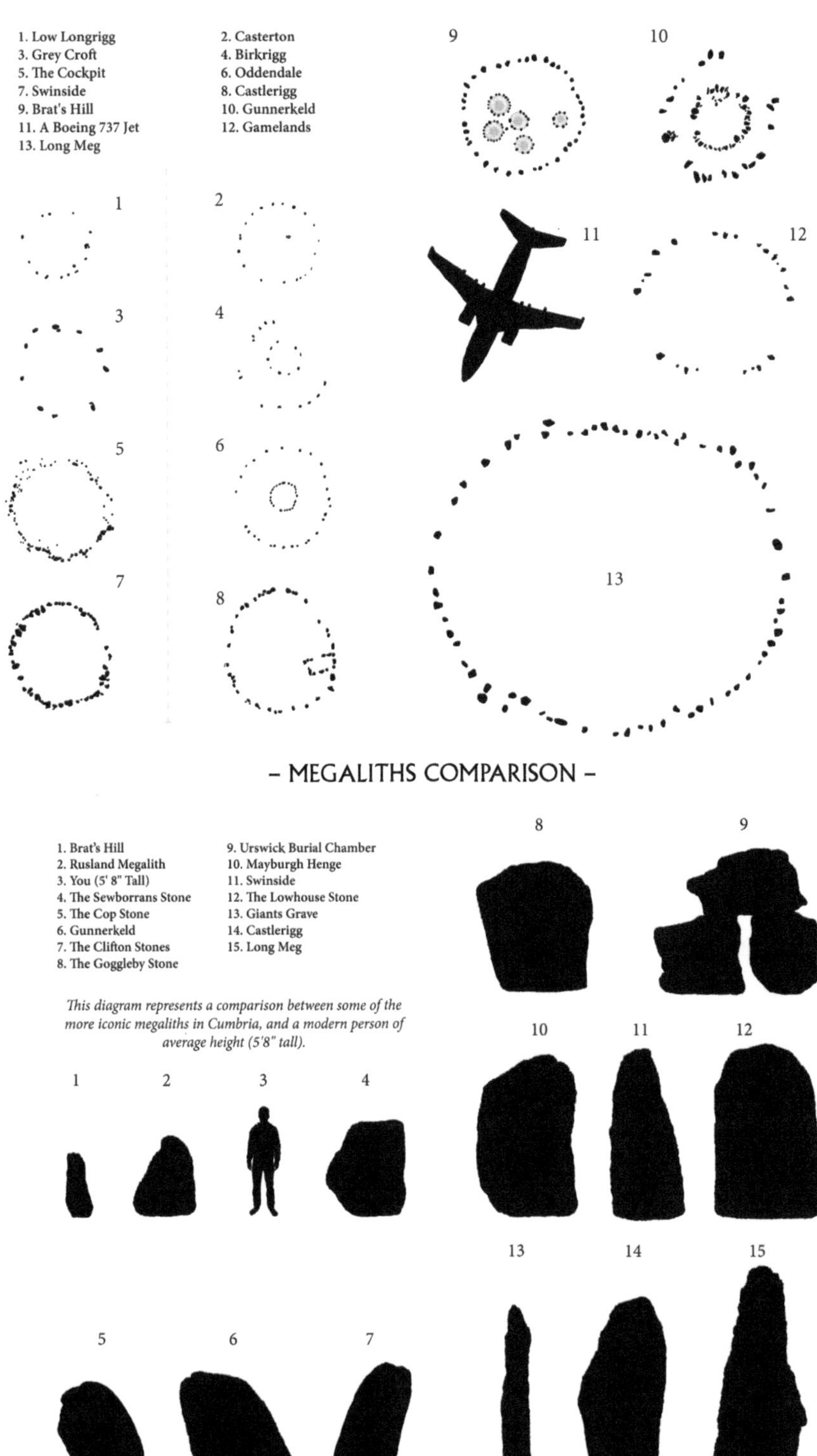

- CUMBRIAN STONE CIRCLES COMPARISON -
1. Low Longrigg
2. Casterton
3. Grey Croft
4. Birkrigg
5. The Cockpit
6. Oddendale
7. Swinside
8. Castlerigg
9. Brat's Hill
10. Gunnerkeld
11. A Boeing 737 Jet
12. Gamelands
13. Long Meg
1
2
3
4
5
6
7
8
9
10
11
12
13
- MEGALITHS COMPARISON -
1. Brat's Hill
2. Rusland Megalith
3. You (5' 8" Tall)
4. The Sewborrans Stone
5. The Cop Stone
6. Gunnerkeld
7. The Clifton Stones
8. The Goggleby Stone
9. Urswick Burial Chamber
10. Mayburgh Henge
11. Swinside
12. The Lowhouse Stone
13. Giants Grave
14. Castlerigg
15. Long Meg
This diagram represents a comparison between some of the more iconic megaliths in Cumbria, and a modern person of average height (5'8" tall).
1
2
3
4
5
6
7
8
9
10
11
12
13
14
15

CARROCK FELL ROUND CAIRNS

The Carrock Fell Round Cairns are found across the moor to the north of Mosedale. The most prominent of these is found at the centre of a hillfort at the peak of Carrock Fell. The views are fine, and the fort is certainly worth the hike.

Down the hill to the east you can find a further three cairns, all of which sit adjacent to the road just south of Carrock Beck. Look for several earth-covered lumps to the east of the road.

GREY YAUDS STONE CIRCLE

Up until the nineteenth century a vast stone circle known as Grey Yauds, consisting of eighty-eight stones, stood in a field near Newbiggin. Unfortunately, the circle was essentially destroyed by farmers, and all that remains is a single standing stone. This stone is said to have been the largest of the circle. Today, it is found deep into private land and is therefore difficult to access.

A LAND BUILT OF STONE, A LAND BUILT OF CULTURE

- IN CONCLUSION -

Cumbria has always been something of a cultural melting pot. It is often wrongly believed that Cumbria is among the least diverse counties in Britain, which is certainly the case when only focusing on modern population demographics. In reality, this assumption fails to factor in those who pass through Cumbria's borders on an almost constant basis. This rain-soaked land served, and continues to serve, as a junction between the four corners of the British Isles. Therefore, a vast number of different cultures pass through the region almost continually. Whether stopping to visit, or simply passing through, no traveller between south-western England and western Scotland, can avoid crossing Cumbria.

This, of course, was no different during prehistory. Britain's geography has remained roughly the same throughout the past 5,500 years. Ireland was always to the west, Scotland was always to the north, and Cumbria was always central. For this reason, it is assumed that people passed through Cumbria en masse throughout prehistory. At sites like Copt Howe, Skelmore Heads and Mayburgh Henge, we can witness an unmistakable dissemination of prehistoric cultures. These new artistic and religious cultures settled like a light snow shower, leaving an impression on the landscape while conforming to its own unique patterns. A wonderful fusion of differing people, coming together to form new and beautiful structures.

Which may be a poignant message to take with you. View your surroundings, appreciate their intricacies; every feature, the small or the large may have been shaped in the unlikeliest of ways, by the unlikeliest of people. It takes a certain level of courage to step out of your comfort zone and question why, exactly, things appear the way they do, which is perhaps the conflict which draws so many to archaeology in the first place. It requires time, patience, perseverance, and sometimes even blind faith, to even begin to draw conclusions on topics as intricate as prehistoric culture. Those Neolithic explorers who first climbed to the peaks of Langdale to quarry would not know the final extent of their endeavour, but by beginning their journey they innovated beyond belief.

While the author would enjoy wrapping this topic in a bow and sending it out to the world with a neat conclusion, there is unfortunately little to conclude here. What he can say with confidence is that the study of the area is far from over, and the unanswered questions on the topic remain open to those who are willing to research. This book should only serve as a broad foundation to the ongoing study of these stones. In reading about every site listed here, you will hopefully have absorbed a body of information which can serve as the groundwork for further study. An immense pool of research on the topic is easily available if you so desire. From which you can begin to formulate theories of your own.

BIBLIOGRAPHY

Anderson, W.D., 'Elva Stone Circle', Cumberland and Westmorland Antiquarian and Archaeological Society (1922).

Barrowclough, D., (2011), *Prehistoric Cumbria* (The History Press, 2009).

Beckensall, S., *Prehistoric Rock Art in Cumbria* (The History Press, 2002).

Bewley, R., *Prehistoric Settlements* (The History Press, 2003).

Bland, J.S., *The Vale of Lyvennet: Its Picturesque Peeps and Legendary Lore* (HardPress, 1910).

Bradley, R., Style, P., Watson, A., 'After the Axes? The Rock Art at Copt Howe, North-west England, and the Neolithic Sequence at Great Langdale, Proceedings of the Prehistoric Society' (2019).

Bradley, R., *The Significance of Monuments* (Routledge, 1999).

Brann, M.L., 'Two Flints from Askham Fell, Cumbria', Cumberland and Westmorland Antiquarian and Archaeological Society (1983).

Brown, F., Griffiths, S., Sheridan, A., Waddington, C., Luke, Y., Dickson, A., Druce, D., Evans, H., Oswald, A., Thomas, J., Frodsham, P., Gibson, A., Fitzpatrick, A., 'The Neolithic Of Northern: England, Annual Conference at Tullie House Museum Carlisle', Proceedings of The Prehistoric Society (2016).

Burl, A., *Four-posters: Bronze Age stone circles of Western Europe* (BAR Publishing, 1988).

Burl, A., *From Carnac to Callanish. The Prehistoric Stone Rows and Avenues of Britain, Ireland and Brittany* (Yale University Press, 1993).

Burl, A., *The Stone Circles of Britain, Ireland, and Brittany* (Yale University Press, 1976).

Champness, C., 'Stainton West CNDR Cumbria Post-excavation Assessment Oxford Archaeology North Birse Civils', Oxford Archaeology (2011).

Clare, F., 'A Beaker burial on Sizergh Fell, near Kendal', Cumberland and Westmorland Antiquarian and Archaeological Society (1953).

Clare, T., 'Recent Work on the Shap 'Avenue', Cumberland and Westmorland Antiquarian and Archaeological Society (1978).

Clare, T., *Prehistoric Monuments of the Lake District* (The History Press, 2007).

sClarkson, T., *Strathclyde: And the Anglo-Saxons in the Viking Age* (Birlinn, 2014).

Clough, T.H., 'Bronze Age metalwork from Cumbria', Cumberland and Westmorland Antiquarian and Archaeological Society (1969).

Clough, T., 'The Beaker period in Cumbria', Cumberland and Westmorland Antiquarian and Archaeological Society (1968).

Collingwood, W.G., 'An Exploration of the Circle on Banniside Moor, Coniston', Cumberland and Westmorland Antiquarian and Archaeological Society (1910).

Collingwood, W.G., 'Tumulus at Grayson-lauds, Glassonby, Cumberland', Cumberland and Westmorland Antiquarian and Archaeological Society (1901).

Cope, J., *The Megalithic European* (Element Books, 2004).

Cowper, H.S., 'Bronze Age Relics from Furness', Cumberland & Westmorland Antiquarian & Archaeological Society (1906).

Cowper, H.S., 'Some Prehistoric Remains in North Lonsdale', Cumberland & Westmorland Antiquarian & Archaeological Society (1887).

Cowper, H.S., 'Unrecorded and Unusual Types of Stone Implements', Cumberland & Westmorland Antiquarian & Archaeological Society (1934).

Cummings, V., *The Neolithic of Britain and Ireland* (Routledge, 2017).

Daw, P.M. 'Bulletin No. 1 Winter / Spring', Stone Circle and Henge Trust (2014).

Dixon, J.A., Fell, C.I., 'Some Bronze Age burial circles at Lacra, near Kirksanton', Cumberland & Westmorland Antiquarian & Archaeological Society (1948).

Dymon, C.W., 'A Group of Cumberland Megaliths', Cumberland & Westmorland Antiquarian & Archaeological Society (1880).

Dymon, C.W., 'An Exploration of 'Sunken Kirk', Swinside, Cumberland, with Incidental Researches in its Neighbourhood', Cumberland & Westmorland Antiquarian & Archaeological Society (1901).

Dymon, C.W., 'Gunnerkeld Stone Circle', Cumberland & Westmorland Antiquarian & Archaeological Society (1880).

Evans, H., Alle, C., Huckerby, E., Seridan, A., Vince, A., 'An early Neolithic occupation site at Holbeck Park Avenue, Barrow-in-Furness', Cumberland and Westmorland Antiquarian and Archaeological Society (2018).

Evans, I.H., 'Prehistoric Landscapes of Cumbria', Doctorate Dissertation, University of Sheffield (2005).

Fairclough, G.J., 'Excavation of standing stones and cairn at Clifton', Cumbria, Cumberland & Westmorland Antiquarian & Archaeological Society (1977).

Ferguson, C., 'On a Tumulus at Old Parks, Kirkoswald: with some Remarks on One at Aspatria, and also on Cup, Ring, and other Rock Markings in Cumberland and Westmorland', Cumberland & Westmorland Antiquarian & Archaeological Society (1894).

Ferguson, R.S., 'Shap Stones' (1899).

Ferguson, R.S., *Stone Circle at Gamelands, Bland House Brow, Township of Raisbeck, Parish of Orton, Westmorland,* Cumberland and Westmorland Antiquarian and Archaeological Society (1881).

Fergusson, J., 'Rude Stone Monuments in All Countries: Their Age and Uses', Cumberland & Westmorland Antiquarian & Archaeological Society (1872).

Frodsham, P., 'Fieldwork module 1c. Phase 2., Long Meg Excavation, Theme 1. Early farmers, Altogether Archaeology' (Durham University, 2015).

Frodsham, P., 'Long Meg and Her Daughters Little Salkeld Cumbria post-excavation full analysis report 4043' (Altogether Archaeology & Durham University, 2016).

Graham, D.J., 'The formation and significance of a moraine-mound complex ('hummocky moraine') of Younger Dryas age in Ennerdale', Institute of Geography and Earth Sciences, University of Wales (2013).

Hallam, D.L., 'Bronze Age Funerary Cups of Northern Britain', University of Bradford eThesis, School of Archaeological Sciences. Faculty of Life Sciences (2015).

Hay, T., 'Threlkeld Settlement', Cumberland and Westmorland Antiquarian and Archaeological Society, (1943).

Hodgeson, K.S., 'Notes' on Stone Circles at Broomrigg', Grey Yauds', Cumberland & Westmorland Antiquarian & Archaeological Society (1934).

Hodgeson, K.S., 'The prehistoric site at Broomrigg near Ainstable: the excavations of 1948–49', Cumberland & Westmorland Antiquarian & Archaeological Society (1950).

Hodgson, K.S., 'Further excavations at Broomrigg near Ainstable, Westmorland Antiquarian and Archaeological Society', Cumberland & Westmorland Antiquarian & Archaeological Society (1952).

Hughes, T.M., 'On another Tumulus on Sizergh Fell', Cumberland and Westmorland Antiquarian and Archaeological Society, (1904).

Jones, A., *The Significance of Colour in European Archaeology* (Berg Publishers, 1999).

Joplin, C.M., 'Druidic Remains in Furness', Archaeologia, or, Miscellaneous tracts relating to antiquity / Society of Antiquaries of London 31 (1846).

Leiden University, 'Between Foraging and Farming: an Extended broad Spectrum of Papers' (2008).

Longworth, I.H., *Collared Urns of the Bronze Age in Great Britain and Ireland* (Cambridge University Press, 1984).

Manby, T.G., 'The distribution of rough-out, 'Cumbrian', and related stone axes of Lake District origin in Northern England', Transactions of the Cumberland and Westmorland Antiquarian and Archaeological Society (1964).

McIntosh, C., *Cambridge Essential English Dictionary* (2011).

Meaden, T., '1 Sept to Friday 6 Sept 2013 at Yewcroft Stone Circle', Selected entries from the travel diary of Terence Meaden (2013).

Meaden, T., *The Secrets of the Avebury Stones* (Souvenir Press, 1999).

Moorhouse, A., 'Stone Implements from the Kirkby Lonsdale District', Cumberland & Westmorland Antiquarian & Archaeological Society (1906).

Pearson, M.P., *The Archaeology of Death and Burial* (The History Press, 2003).

Pipe B., Pipe, S., *Historic Cumbria: Off the Beaten Track* (Amberley Publishing, 2015).

Pollard, J., *Neolithic Britain* (Shire Publications, 2002).

Pryor, F., *Home: A Time Traveller's Tales from Britain's Prehistory* (Penguin, 2018).

Quartermaine, J., Claris, P., 'The Neolithic quarries and axe factory sites of Great Langdale and Scafell Pike', Proceedings of the Prehistoric Society (1989).

Robb, J., 'Art (Pre)History: Ritual, Narrative and Visual Culture in Neolithic and Bronze Age Europe', Journal of Archaeological Method and Theory (2020).

Roberts, C.R., Mitchell, C.W., *Spring Mounds in Southern Tunisia,* Geological Society, London, Special Publication (1987).

Sievekin, G., 'Excavation of a Stone Circle at Wilson Scar, Shap North', Cumberland & Westmorland Antiquarian & Archaeological Society (1952).

Simpson, J., 'Shap Stones', Cumberland & Westmorland Antiquarian & Archaeological Society (1898).

Simpson, J., 'Stone Circles near Shap, Westmorland', Cumberland & Westmorland Antiquarian & Archaeological Society (1883).

Spence J.E., 'An Early Settlement on Moor Divock', Cumberland & Westmorland Antiquarian & Archaeological Society (1933).

Style, P., 'Polished axes, Petroglyphs and Pathways', University of Central Lancashire undergraduate dissertation (2009).

Style, P., 'Prehistoric Enclosures in the Rydal Valley', Cumberland and Westmorland Antiquarian and Archaeological Society (2012).

Style, P., 'Yet more Prehistoric Rock Art, a Settlement and Cairn-field near Rydal', Cumberland and Westmorland Antiquarian and Archaeological Society (2016).

Taylor, M.W., 'The Prehistoric Remains on Moordivock, near Ullswater', Cumberland & Westmorland Antiquarian & Archaeological Society (1885).

Thomas, J., 'On the Origins and Development of Cursus Monuments in Britain, Proceedings of the Prehistoric Society' (2006).

Topping, P., 'The Penrith Henges: A Survey by the Royal Commission on the Historical Monuments of England', Proceedings of the Prehistoric Society (1992).

Turnbull, P., Walsh, D., 'A Beaker Burial in Levens Park', Cumberland and Westmorland Antiquarian and Archaeological Society (1996).

Turnbull, P., Walsh, D., 'A Prehistoric Ritual Sequence at Oddendale, Near Shap', Cumberland & Westmorland Antiquarian & Archaeological Society (1997).

Turner, V.E., 'Results of survey work carried out between the Shap and Askham Fells, Cumbria', Cumberland and Westmorland Antiquarian and Archaeological Society (1991).

Valdez-Tullett, J., *Design and Connectivity: The Case of Atlantic Rock Art* (BAR Publishing, 2019).

Vyner, B., 'The Tortie Stone Revisited', Cumberland & Westmorland Antiquarian & Archaeological Society (2013).

Waley, D., *A Dictionary of Lake District Place-Names* (English Place-Name Society, 2006).

Watson, D., *A Guide to the Stone Circles of the Lake District* (Simple Guides, 2009).

Archaeological Record Sourcing

Transactions of the Cumberland and Westmorland Antiquarian & Archaeological Society. [Accessed at https://archaeologydataservice.ac.uk]

Historic England's listed sites map, [viewable at www.historicengland.org.uk/listing/the-list/map-search

Pastscape database, viewable at www.pastscape.org.uk]

Heritage Gateway, [viewable at www.heritagegateway.org.uk]

Inventory of the Historical Monuments in Westmorland, [viewable at www.british-history.ac.uk/rchme/westm]

User submitted database at Megalithic Portal, [view at www.megalithic.co.uk]

National Trust Hertage Records Map, [viewable at https://heritagerecords.nationaltrust.org.uk/map]

Webpage Sources

Aaron Watson, excellent fieldwork journals and photographs, [viewable at www.aaronwatson.co.uk]

The Smell of Water, viewable at [https://teessidepsychogeography.wordpress.com]

Aerial imagery/crop marks studied using Google Maps/My Maps, [viewable at www.googlemaps.com]

An Inventory of the Historical Monuments in Westmorland 1936: viewable at www.british-history.ac.uk/rchme/westm

English Heritage Castlerigg tourist information, [viewable at www.english-heritage.org.uk/visit/places/castlerigg-stone-circle/history]

Fell Rangers, National Trust [http://fellrangers.blogspot.com/2013/07/rock-art-in-great-langdale-and-grasmere.html]

Footpath and access confirmation, [viewable at https://footpathmap.co.uk]

Funerary Cairn (Sampson's Bratfull), National Trust, [viewable at: https://heritagerecords.nationaltrust.org.uk/HBSMR/MonRecord.aspx?uid=MNA118518]

Historic Environment Scotland Rock Art, viewable at [www.rockart.scot/about-rock-art/rock-art-of-britain-and-ireland]

'Langdale axes: Cumbria's prehistoric export', Diane McIlmoyle, 2011, [https://esmeraldamac.wordpress.com/2011/05/11/cumbrias-first-export-langdale-axes]

Map showing the stone rows identified by M.W. Taylor. (Source: Taylor, 1886), viewable at [https://archaeologydataservice.ac.uk/archiveDS/archiveDownload?t=arch-2055-1/dissemination/pdf/Article_Level_Pdf/tcwaas/001/1886/vol8/tcwaas_001_1886_vol8_0036.pdf]

Shap Historic Google My Maps guide, [at: www.google.com/maps/d/viewer?msa=0&hl=en&ie=UTF8&ll=54.56198821291965 per cent2C-2.6889048507238l6&spn=0.07579 per cent2C0.105189&t=h&source=embed&dg=feature&mid=1dPOCohGFf-awyUbOTiV3o0xwg2o&z=17]

Shap Historical Society, viewable at [https://shaphistoricsites.wordpress.com/prehistory/standing-stones-stone-cirlces/gunnerkeld-stone-circle]

Stone Circles in Cumbria, History Magazine, viewable at [www.historic-uk.com/HistoryMagazine/DestinationsUK/Stone-Circles-in-Cumbria]

The Friends of The Ullswater Way [www.ullswaterway.co.uk/cockpit.html]

Visit Cumbria Stone Circles, viewable at [www.visitcumbria.com/stone-circle]

Scott, T., 'Ley Lines and Avebury Henge, the Better Version of Stonehenge', [viewable at www.youtube.com/watch?v=LGwgT5jho6I]

NATIONAL GRID REFERENCES

THE CENTRAL LAKES

Langdale

The Langdale Axe Factory – NY 27428 07231

Side Pike Cups – NY 28634 05590

Copt Howe – NY 31399 05834

Grasmere

Allan Bank Cup–marked Rock – NY 33402 07695

Broadgate Park Cup–marked Rock – NY 33857 07776

Dunmail Raise – NY 32725 11708

Rydal Cairns – N/A

Low Kingate Stone Cirlce – NY 41630 05918

Wythburn Cups Marks – NY 32049 12578

North Lakes

Elva Plain Stone Circle – NY 17699 31713

Castlerigg Stone Circle – NY 29142 23628

Bleaberry Haws

Bleaberry Cairn B– SD 26739 94488

Bleaberry Cairn C – SD 26788 94429

Bleaberry Cairn E – SD 26562 94714

Bleaberry Cairn G – SD 26600 94958

Bleaberry Haws Stone Circle – SD 26567 94915

Other Sites in the Lake District

Rusland Menhir – SD 33085 88668

Four Stones Hill Standing Stones – NY 48955 16199

Patterdale Cup Markings – NY 40029 15784

Hartsop Round Cairn – NY 39846 11673

Bannishead Enclosure (The Rigg) – SD 27701 96095

THE IRISH SEA

Burnmoor

Boot Kerb Cairn – NY 17635 01896

Brat's Hill Stone Circle – NY 17373 02342

White Moss Stone Circles – NY 17274 02404

Low Longrigg SW – NY 17251 02783

Low Longrigg NE – NY 17284 02814

Furness

Birkrigg Stone Circle – SD 29236 73966

Skelmore Heads Long Barrow – SD 27430 75404

Great Urswick Burial Chamber – SD 26270 74469

St Bees

Grey Croft Stone Circle – NY 03332 02378

Yewcroft Stone Circle – NY 04311 10648

Kinniside Stone Circle – NY 06011 14035

Studfold Stone Circle – NY 04005 22356

Millom

The Giant's Grave – SD 13614 81103

Swinside Stone Circle – SD 17163 88176

Lacra Bank

Lacra A – SD 14990 81327

Lacra B – SD 14920 80986

Lacra C – SD 15013 80969

Lacra Avenue / Lacra D – SD 15119 81252

Other Sites on the Cumbrian Coast

Ash House Stones – SD 19286 87291

Blake Fell Round Cairns – NY 11714 20320

Gretigate Stone Circles – NY 05796 03665

Kirkby Moor Round Cairn – SD 25143 82995

Knapperthaw Stone Circle – SD 28002 84239

Mecklin Park Cairn Field – NY 12964 01842

Sampsons Bratful – NY 09842 08053

The Kirk – SD 25076 82750

The Priapus Stone – SD 26757 74146

Whitrow Beck Stone Circle – SD 13422 93866

SOUTH CUMBRIA

Levens Park

Levens Park Ring Cairn – SD 50513 86175

Levens Henge – SD 49744 85863

Sizergh Fell Round Cairn – SD 49524 86866

Casterton

Brownthwaite Pike Round Cairn – SD 64766 80479

Casterton Stone Circle – SD 63934 79994

EASTERN CUMBRIA

Shap

Skellaw Hill – NY 55652 15467

Goggleby Stone – NY 55924 15093

The Giant's Foot – NY 56299 14781

Kemp Howe – NY 56800 13303

White Raise (Shap) – NY 53469 13438

Crosby Ravensworth

Castlehowe Scar – NY 58751 15471

Iron Hill – NY 59635 14825

Oddendale – NY 59201 12910

Kalmott Cairn – NY 59290 13330

White Hag – NY 60724 11598

White Hag Cairn – NY 61024 11582

Long Scar Pike Round Cairn – NY 59335 10867

Moor Divock

Cop Stone – NY 49602 21597

Askham Fell Ring Cairn – NY 49403 21961

Moor Divock 5 – NY 49308 22187

White Raise (Moor Divock) – NY 48877 22446

The Cockpit – NY 48273 22241

Knipe Scar

Gunnerkeld Stone Circle – NY 56823 17752

Shapbeck Stone Circle – NY 55273 18861

Knipe Scar Round Cairn – NY 53189 19437

Knipe Scar Stone Circle – NY 52880 19304

Asby Scar

Gamelands Stone Circle – NY 64003 08165

Raiset Pike – NY 68399 07254

Other Sites in Eastern Cumbria

Stone Howe – NY 54469 14909

Swarth Fell Stone Circle – NY 45696 19005

Hardendale Stone Circle – NY 57320 12357

Hardendale Nab – NY 58144 14015

The Thunder Stone – NY 58176 15610

Penhurrock Cairn – NY 62877 10444

Castle Folds Round Cairn – NY 65265 08967

PENRITH

Eamont Bridge

Clifton Stones – NY 53141 25932

Mayburgh Henge – NY 51919 28433

KART – NY 52335 28385

Low Moor Long Barrow – NY 53697 24316

Lowhouse Stone – NY 49628 34350

Sewborrans Stone – NY 48849 29996

Mossthorne Long Cairn – NY 48286 30435

Broomrigg Plantation

Broomrigg A – NY 54800 46697

Broomrigg B – NY 54851 46600

Broomrigg C – NY 54819 46460

Broomrigg I – NY 54740 46557

Eden Valley

Long Meg and Her Daughters – NY 57113 37210

Little Meg – NY 57696 37481

Glassonby – NY 57279 39350

Other Sites Near Penrith

Carrock Fell Round Cairn – NY 34332 33638

Green Howe Bowl Barrow – NY 26082 38148

Leacet Hill Stone Circle – NY 56256 26310